Windows 7: Up and Running

Windows 7: Up and Running

Wei-Meng Lee

O'REILLY®

Beijing · Cambridge · Farnham · Köln · Sebastopol · Taipei · Tokyo

Windows 7: Up and Running
by Wei-Meng Lee

Copyright © 2010 Wei-Meng Lee. All rights reserved.
Printed in the United States of America.

Published by O'Reilly Media, Inc., 1005 Gravenstein Highway North, Sebastopol, CA 95472.

O'Reilly books may be purchased for educational, business, or sales promotional use. Online editions are also available for most titles (*http://my.safaribooksonline.com*). For more information, contact our corporate/institutional sales department: (800) 998-9938 or *corporate@oreilly.com*.

Editors: Brian Jepson and Laurel Ruma
Production Editor: Sumita Mukherji
Copyeditor: Nancy Kotary
Proofreader: Sumita Mukherji

Indexer: Fred Brown
Cover Designer: Karen Montgomery
Interior Designer: David Futato
Illustrator: Robert Romano

Printing History:

October 2009:   First Edition.

ISBN: 978-0-596-80404-6

[M]

1253635580

Table of Contents

Preface ix

1. **Installing Windows 7** 1
   Versions of Windows 7   1
      System Requirements   3
   Installing Windows 7   4
      What's New in Windows 7   9
   Summary   17

2. **Getting Around Windows 7** 19
   Taskbar   19
      Aero Peek   20
      Pinning Applications to the Taskbar   21
      Jump Lists   22
   Libraries   26
      Exploring Libraries   26
      Creating Your Own Library   27
   Desktop Gadgets   31
   Summary   35

3. **File Sharing** 37
   HomeGroup   37
      Creating a New HomeGroup   39
      Joining a HomeGroup   43
      Sharing Files   43
      Sharing Printers   43
      Streaming Music   46
   File Sharing with Windows XP   47
   File Sharing with Mac OS X   50
   Summary   51

4. Security **53**

Action Center   53

User Account Control   57

The Credential Manager   59

    Using the Credential Manager   60

    Linking Online IDs   61

    Backing Up the Credentials   63

BitLocker Drive Encryption   64

    BitLocker   65

    BitLocker To Go   67

Encrypting File System (NTFS Encryption)   69

    Creating Certificates   71

    Importing Certificates   73

Antispyware and Firewall Applications   73

    Windows Defender   73

    Windows Firewall   75

Summary   77

5. Essential Applications **79**

Windows Live Essentials   79

    Windows Live Messenger   80

    Windows Live Mail   81

    Windows Live Photo Gallery   87

    Windows Live Writer   88

    Windows Live Family Safety   89

    Windows Live Movie Maker   91

Built-in Applications   92

    Snipping Tool   92

    Sound Recorder   94

    Windows PowerShell   95

    Windows Photo Viewer   97

    Windows Disc Image Burner   99

    Windows Media Center   101

    Math Input Panel   103

    XPS Viewer   104

    Sticky Notes   105

    Calculator   105

    Microsoft WordPad   107

    Microsoft Paint   107

    Windows Media Player 12   107

Summary   108

6. **Internet Explorer 8** **109**
    Usability   109
      Smart Address Bar   110
      Enhanced Tabbed Browsing and Grouping   110
      Compatibility View   112
      Find on Page   113
      Improved Search   114
      Web Slices   116
      Accelerators   120
    Privacy   121
      InPrivate Browsing   122
      InPrivate Filtering   123
      Suggested Sites   125
    Security   127
      Domain Highlighting   127
      SmartScreen Filter   128
    Summary   130

7. **Using Windows XP Mode** **131**
    Installing Windows XP Mode   131
      Using Windows XP Mode   132
    Running Windows XP Mode Seamlessly with Windows 7   135
      USB Mode   137
    Installing Other Operating Systems   138
      Creating a New Virtual Machine   138
      Starting the New Virtual Machine   139
    Summary   142

8. **Windows 7 Tips and Tricks** **143**
    Customizing the UI   143
      Change Windows Explorer's Default View   143
      Open a Command Window Anywhere   147
      Use Themes for Other Locations   148
      Touch Gestures   150
      Auto-Login   151
    Taskbar   152
      Rearranging the Icons in the Taskbar   153
      Displaying the Old Quick Launch Bar   153
      Taskbar Shortcuts   154
      Pinning Folders to the Taskbar   157
    Utilities/Troubleshooting Tools   157
      Projector Screen Selection   157
      Problems Steps Recorder   158

Troubleshooting Sleep Mode Problems   159
Windows Disk Image Burner   162
Calibrating Your Display   163
Windows 7 Compatibility Mode   164
Installing Windows 7   167
Installing Windows 7 Using a USB Hard Drive   167
Installing Windows 7 Using a USB Thumb Drive   170
Dual Booting Windows 7 with Windows Vista and Windows XP   171
Installing Windows 7 on a Virtual Hard Disk (VHD) File   172
Summary   177

Index 179

Preface

Windows 7 is Microsoft's latest version of its Windows operating system. Unlike its predecessor, Vista, Windows 7 offers incremental upgrades and is aimed at ensuring maximum compatibility with applications and hardware already supported in Vista. Microsoft's key agenda around Windows 7 is to woo many of the Windows XP users who skipped Vista.

Windows 7 offers significant performance improvements over its predecessors—most notably Windows Vista and Windows XP. It is still based on the Vista kernel, but comes with a redesigned Windows shell, a new taskbar, and a less-annoying User Account Control (UAC) system. There are also improvements in networking, in particular the introduction of a home network system known as *HomeGroup*.

This compact book offers the quickest path for Windows XP and Vista users to get started with Microsoft's new Windows 7 operating system. Microsoft has learned from the mistakes of Windows Vista, and Windows 7 shows it—this new OS is much faster and more stable. Millions of people have tried the public beta and Windows 7 Release Candidate, and many give the software high marks.

Windows 7: Up and Running helps you be productive immediately. You'll learn what's new and what's changed, as well as everything you need to get going, from installing to configuring the system. Windows 7 is poised to be a big hit among PC users, and with this handy guide, you can be up and running with this new operating system right away.

This book will help you:

- Quickly learn the system's user interface, including the taskbar, Jump Lists, Desktop Gadgets, Aero Shake, system tray, and more.
- Discover the joys of networking with HomeGroup and file sharing, along with improved Wi-Fi usability.

- Take a tour of the system's improved security, including the Action Center, User Account Control, and the Credential Manager.

- Learn how to use Windows Live Essentials for messaging, photo sharing, movie making, email, and blogging.

- Get to know the built-in applications and utilities, such as IE8, Windows Media Player 12, Microsoft Paint, and WordPad.

How This Book Is Organized

The chapters in this book are organized as follows:

Chapter 1, *Installing Windows 7*
This chapter first walks you through the different versions of Windows 7 available, and then gives you an overview of the installation process. You will then take a look at some of the new features in Windows 7 before we examine them in detail in subsequent chapters.

Chapter 2, *Getting Around Windows 7*
Among the new features (see Chapter 1) are the much improved taskbar, the improved capabilities of gadgets, as well as the many UI improvements that make the Windows experience a much more enjoyable one. In this chapter, you will take a more detailed look at three features that have the greatest effect on your daily Windows experience: taskbar, Libraries, and Desktop Gadgets.

Chapter 3, *File Sharing*
File sharing has been one of the common features across all Windows operating systems. Besides sharing files with other Windows computers, the file sharing feature in Windows 7 also allows users to share files with other non-Windows computers, such as those running Mac OS X and Linux. In Windows 7, file sharing has been further simplified with the new HomeGroup feature. In this chapter, you will learn about the HomeGroup feature, as well as learn how to share files with other computers on the network.

Chapter 4, *Security*
On the security front, Windows 7 has streamlined several features found in Windows Vista, making them much more accessible and less irritating in this new version of Windows. For example, the infamous UAC is one of the most irritating features in Vista. In this version of Windows, Microsoft has tweaked UAC so that it interrupts users only when needed. Microsoft has also replaced the Security Center in Vista with the new Action Center in Windows 7, which focuses not just on displaying problems, but also on offering suggestions and solutions to solve problems. The Credential Manager now has the ability to back up its credential information to a file. In addition, Enterprise and Ultimate users can now encrypt a portable thumb drive using BitLocker To Go.

Chapter 5, *Essential Applications*

One of the longstanding Windows traditions that Windows 7 broke is related to bundled applications: it contains far fewer bundled applications than did previous versions. For example, Microsoft Mail will not be available when you install Windows 7. Similarly, Messenger will also not be available when you install Windows 7. Instead, Microsoft will offer a suite of essential applications as a separate download. Doing so allows Microsoft to have separate release timelines for Windows and these essential applications. This also allows it to make these essential applications available for earlier versions of Windows more easily. In the first part of this chapter, you will first see how you can install the suite of essential applications from Microsoft free of charge. You will then look at the suite of built-in applications that ship with Windows 7.

Chapter 6, *Internet Explorer 8*

Windows 7 ships with the new Internet Explorer 8 (IE8). IE8 builds on the foundation of IE7, and this latest release contains many useful enhancements in the areas of usability, privacy, and security. In this chapter, you will learn about some of the innovations in IE8 and how they affect the way you surf the Web.

Chapter 7, *Using Windows XP Mode*

When Microsoft introduced Windows Vista, many users were very upset, as they discovered that some of their older applications could not work correctly in Vista (some application vendors simply did not upgrade their applications for Vista, or charged more for new versions than users were happy to pay). As such, a lot of users (and businesses) cited this as a reason for not upgrading to Vista. Microsoft realizes the severity of this problem and hopes to solve this problem in Windows 7 by providing a feature known as Windows XP Mode (XPM). XPM lets you run your legacy Windows XP applications inside a virtualized environment, either from within a virtual XP window or as a seamlessly integrated application within Windows 7.

Chapter 8, *Windows 7 Tips and Tricks*

Windows 7 is a complex operating system that is more evolutionary than revolutionary. A lot of features available in Windows 7 are based on the features available in the earlier versions of Windows: XP and Vista. Nevertheless, Windows 7 contains a wealth of new features that greatly improve the usability of Windows and its performance. In this chapter, you will learn some of the tips and tricks to getting the most out of Windows 7.

Who This Book Is For

This book is written primarily for existing users of Microsoft Windows operating systems who are interested in upgrading to Windows 7. In particular, I am assuming that you are at least familiar with Windows XP or Windows Vista (or both). If you are a new user coming to Windows 7 from another platform (such as Mac OS X or Linux), you will still find this book easy to follow.

Conventions Used in This Book

The following typographical conventions are used in this book:

Italic
> Indicates new terms, URLs, email addresses, filenames, and file extensions.

`Constant width`
> Used for program listings, as well as within paragraphs to refer to program elements such as variable or function names, databases, data types, environment variables, statements, and keywords.

`Constant width bold`
> Shows commands or other text that should be typed literally by the user.

`Constant width italic`
> Shows text that should be replaced with user-supplied values or by values determined by context.

 This icon signifies a tip, suggestion, or general note.

 This icon signifies a warning or caution.

Using Code Examples

This book is here to help you get your job done. In general, you may use the code in this book in your programs and documentation. You do not need to contact us for permission unless you're reproducing a significant portion of the code. For example, writing a program that uses several chunks of code from this book does not require permission. Selling or distributing a CD-ROM of examples from O'Reilly books does require permission. Answering a question by citing this book and quoting example code does not require permission. Incorporating a significant amount of example code from this book into your product's documentation does require permission.

We appreciate, but do not require, attribution. An attribution usually includes the title, author, publisher, and ISBN. For example: "*Windows 7: Up and Running* by Wei-Meng Lee. Copyright 2010 Wei-Meng Lee, 978-0-596-80404-6."

If you feel your use of code examples falls outside fair use or the permission given here, feel free to contact us at *permissions@oreilly.com*.

How to Contact Us

Please address comments and questions concerning this book to the publisher:

O'Reilly Media, Inc.
1005 Gravenstein Highway North
Sebastopol, CA 95472
800-998-9938 (in the United States or Canada)
707-829-0515 (international or local)
707-829-0104 (fax)

We have a web page for this book, where we list errata, examples, and any additional information. You can access this page at:

http://oreilly.com/catalog/9780596804046

To comment or ask technical questions about this book, send email to:

bookquestions@oreilly.com

For more information about our books, conferences, Resource Centers, and the O'Reilly Network, see our website at:

http://oreilly.com

Safari® Books Online

 Safari Books Online is an on-demand digital library that lets you easily search over 7,500 technology and creative reference books and videos to find the answers you need quickly.

With a subscription, you can read any page and watch any video from our library online. Read books on your cell phone and mobile devices. Access new titles before they are available for print, and get exclusive access to manuscripts in development and post feedback for the authors. Copy and paste code samples, organize your favorites, download chapters, bookmark key sections, create notes, print out pages, and benefit from tons of other time-saving features.

O'Reilly Media has uploaded this book to the Safari Books Online service. To have full digital access to this book and others on similar topics from O'Reilly and other publishers, sign up for free at *http://my.safaribooksonline.com*.

Acknowledgments

My sincere thanks to my editor, Brian Jepson, for suggesting that we do a book on Microsoft's latest operating system—Windows 7. Although many users were not too thrilled with Windows Vista, the early beta and candidate releases of Windows 7 took many critics by surprise. Not only does Windows 7 come with some really nice features, but more importantly, it was a very stable operating system that performs well even with older hardware. Realizing the potentials of Windows 7, I was very excited when I got the chance to work on this book—especially with Brian, who has been more of a mentor to me than an editor. Thanks, Brian!

I would also like to thank O'Reilly Managing Editor Marlowe Shaeffer. She has been instrumental in getting the book ready so that you can get this book in your hands before Windows 7 ships. Thank you, Marlowe.

Last but not least, I want to thank my family for their love and support, especially my wife, SzeWa, and our lovely dog, Ookii. I love you all!

And of course, a big thank you to the production crew at O'Reilly, who made this book possible.

CHAPTER 1

Installing Windows 7

Windows 7 is Microsoft's latest version of its Windows operating system. Unlike its predecessor, Vista, Windows 7 offers incremental upgrades and is aimed at ensuring maximum compatibility with applications and hardware already supported in Vista. As mentioned in the Preface, Microsoft's key agenda regarding Windows 7 is to lure back many of the Windows XP users who skipped Vista.

Windows 7 offers significant performance improvements over its predecessors—most notably Windows Vista and Windows XP. It is still based on the Vista kernel, but comes with substantial performance improvements and a redesigned Windows shell, a new taskbar, and a less-annoying User Account Control (UAC) system. There are also improvements in networking, in particular the introduction of a home network system known as *HomeGroup*.

This chapter first walks you through the different versions of Windows 7 available, followed by an overview of the installation process. We will then take a look at some of the new features in Windows 7 before we get into them in detail in subsequent chapters.

Versions of Windows 7

With Windows Vista, Microsoft released multiple editions of its operating system with the intention of targeting different segments of its user base with different features at different price points. However, this approach wasn't well received, as it confused the market; many users urged Microsoft to come up with one simple, all-encompassing version of the operating system.

With Windows 7, Microsoft still has many editions. However, Microsoft is expected to focus its marketing effort on just two editions—Home Premium and Professional—just as it did with Windows XP. Here is a list of the available editions, in ascending order, from least to most advanced:

Starter Edition

A lightweight edition for netbook computers. *Netbooks* are low-powered computers specifically designed for lightweight tasks such as web browsing and emailing. In this edition, Windows 7 will lack more advanced features such as Media Center, Aero Glass, fast user switching, multiple-monitor support, DVD playback, and multitouch support. This edition is geared toward replacing Windows XP on inexpensive computers such as netbooks, a market that is currently dominated by Windows XP. This edition will likely be available only as a preinstallation by OEMs.

Windows 7 Starter Edition Application Limits?

In the early beta days of Windows 7, Microsoft announced that Windows 7 Starter Edition would have a three-application limit. That is, no more than three applications could run at the same time. Apparently, this did not go over well with the public, and Microsoft reversed the decision.

Some restrictions remain. Microsoft has disabled the Personalize option in the context menu that is shown when you right-click the desktop. This means that you won't be able to change your wallpaper. This limitation might be to allow OEMs to provide their own custom-branded wallpapers. At press time, it is unclear whether Microsoft will lift this limitation as well. To me, it makes perfect sense to lift this limitation—how can you call your computer a Personal Computer when you can't even change your wallpaper?

Home Basic

This edition is designated for emerging markets only; it is for customers who are looking for an inexpensive entry-level Windows experience (limited Aero support, no features such as Windows Media Center or multitouch support).

Home Premium

This edition is designed for home users and will include features like Media Center, multitouch support, the Aero Glass UI, and so on.

Professional

This edition is designed for home workers and small businesses, and will include features like advanced network backup and the Encrypting File System.

Enterprise

Includes everything that Professional includes and adds BitLocker protection. It will have the option to encrypt USB flash drives and external hard disks. It also includes DirectAccess, which allows remote workers to access a company network securely without using a VPN, and federated search.

Ultimate

Includes all the features available in Windows 7.

Windows 7 Ultimate edition is really the same as the Enterprise edition. The key difference is that the Enterprise edition will be sold through volume licensing to companies, as well as through the Software Assurance program. The Ultimate edition, however, will be available to retail customers.

One key thing to note about the different editions of Windows 7 is that each higher edition is a superset of its lower edition. That is, all the features available in Starter Edition will be available on the Home Basic edition, and the Home Premium edition will include all the features of Home Basic, and so on. This is different from Vista, where Media Center was included in the Home Premium edition but not available in the Business edition.

Though there are six different editions of Windows 7, Microsoft will focus its marketing effort on just the Home Premium, Professional, and Ultimate editions. This is very similar to Windows XP, in which you have only two main editions—Home and Professional. As a quick rule of thumb, Windows 7 Home Premium is targeted at consumers and Professional is targeted at small businesses.

System Requirements

If you are currently running Windows Vista, the good news is that you are ready for Windows 7. Tests performed by various parties have consistently confirmed that Windows 7 outperformed Windows Vista on a similar hardware configuration.

If you are coming from previous versions of Windows (pre-Vista), take note of the following *suggested* hardware requirements:

- 1 GHz or faster 32-bit or 64-bit processor
- 1 GB RAM (for 32-bit) or 2 GB RAM (for 64-bit)
- 16 GB of available disk space (for 32-bit) or 20 GB of available disk space (for 64-bit)
- DirectX 9 graphics device with Windows Display Driver Model 1.0 or higher (for Aero—the graphical user interface and default theme in most editions of Windows 7)

Though it is suggested that you have at least 1 GB of RAM, Windows 7 runs perfectly on my old trusty Dell Inspiron 5150 notebook (a 3 GHz Pentium 4 processor with 640 MB of RAM). The suggested requirements are necessary to experience all the features of Windows 7 (such as Aero Glass effects), but Windows 7 will still function on lesser hardware.

Installing Windows 7

If you are currently running Windows Vista (with Service Pack 1), you can upgrade to Windows 7 directly from within Vista. Windows XP users will need to install a fresh copy of Windows 7.

Upgrading from Windows XP to Windows 7

Although Windows XP users cannot upgrade directly to Windows 7, Microsoft provides the Windows Easy Transfer utility, which allows you to easily transfer your computer's settings and files to the new Windows 7.

To launch the Windows Easy Transfer utility, log in to Windows XP, insert the Windows 7 installation disc, and navigate to the *\support\migwiz* folder. Double-click *migwiz.exe* to launch the Windows Easy Transfer utility (see Figure 1-1). Follow the instructions on the screen to save the settings to another computer via a cable or network, or save them to a hard disk or USB drive.

When Windows 7 has been installed, you can run the Windows Easy Transfer utility via Start→All Programs→Accessories→System Tools→Windows Easy Transfer. Follow the online instructions to copy the saved settings onto the new Windows 7 installation.

Figure 1-1. Use Windows Easy Transfer to migrate your Windows XP settings to Windows 7

The following steps will walk you through the process of installing Windows 7 on a fresh computer.

Installing Windows 7 is straightforward—if you're doing a clean install, simply boot up your computer with the Windows 7 installation DVD inside the DVD drive and instruct your computer to boot from the DVD (you may need to press a key, such as F11 or F12, while the computer is starting to enter the boot selection screen). If you're upgrading, simply boot into Windows Vista, insert the disc, and run the installer (if you are using Windows XP, see the previous sidebar "Upgrading from Windows XP to Windows 7").

When the installer has booted up, you will be greeted with the screen shown in Figure 1-2 (the upgrade screen is slightly different; you will have an option to check the compatibility of your system or start the installation). You will be asked to select the language to install, the time and currency format, and your keyboard type.

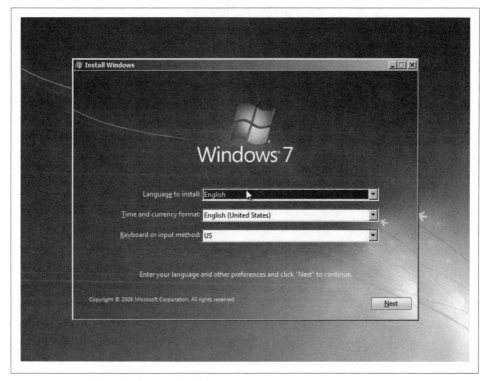

Figure 1-2. Installing Windows 7: the first step

With the selections made, you can now install Windows 7 by clicking the "Install now" button (see Figure 1-3).

You will be asked to accept the license agreement. (If you are upgrading, you'll first have the option to go online to get any updates to the installer first.) Check the licensing checkbox and continue.

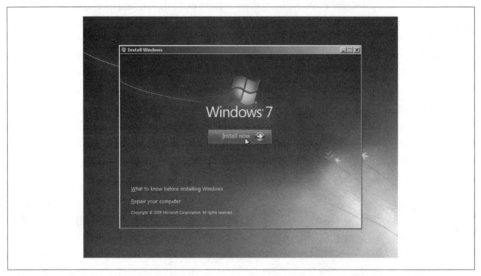

Figure 1-3. Click the "Install now" button to start the Windows 7 installation process

On the next screen, you have a choice between upgrading your existing Windows or installing a fresh copy of Windows. If you are using Windows XP or earlier, the first option will not work for you—select the Custom (advanced) option (see Figure 1-4).

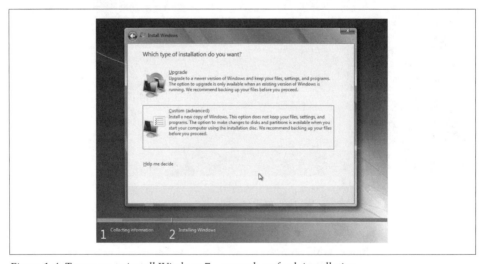

Figure 1-4. Two ways to install Windows 7—upgrade or fresh installation

You can upgrade from Windows Vista only if you run the installer from within Windows Vista. If you do a fresh boot using the Windows 7 installation disc, you will not be able to upgrade (you will be asked to rerun the installation from within Windows).

For a fresh installation, you will be asked to select a disk for installing Windows 7. Select the appropriate disk and click Next (see Figure 1-5). If you are upgrading, the Windows 7 installer will generate a compatibility report and save it to your desktop.

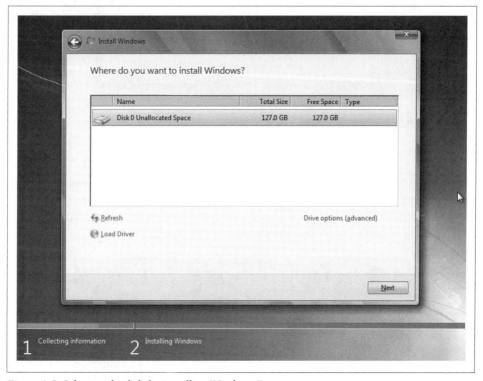

Figure 1-5. Selecting the disk for installing Windows 7

 If you are doing a clean install via the Custom (advanced) option, be sure to back up any important data you have previously saved on your hard drive before starting the installation. Installing Windows 7 will wipe out all previous data.

Windows will now take some time to copy all the files into the selected disk and proceed with the installation (see Figure 1-6). This will take about 20–30 minutes, depending on the speed of your computer.

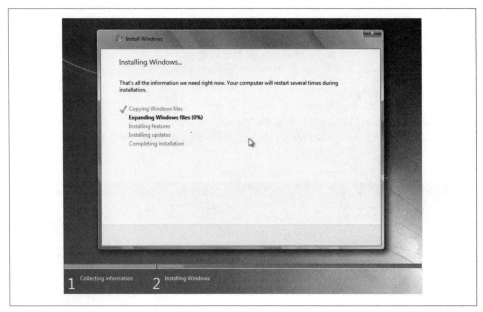

Figure 1-6. Windows 7 proceeding with the installation

When the installation is complete, Windows 7 will restart. After Windows 7 has been restarted, you should see the screen shown in Figure 1-7. Provide a username; your computer name will be created based on what you have entered (you can change it to another name if you want to after the installation). Click Next.

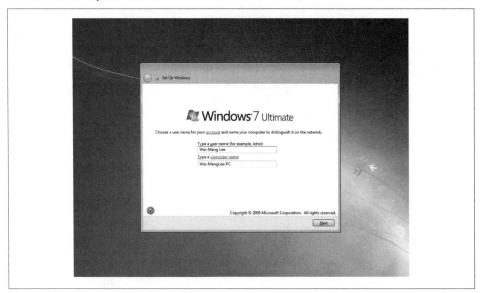

Figure 1-7. Providing a username for your account

You will be asked to enter a password to protect your user account. You are strongly advised to provide one. In the next screen, you will be asked to enter a product key to activate Windows 7.

You will also be asked to select a way to update Windows. I suggest that you select the first option, "Use recommended settings"; see Figure 1-8.

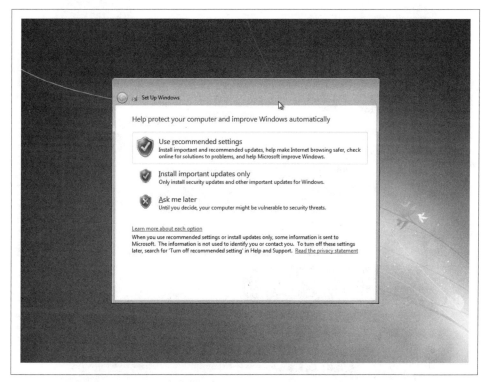

Figure 1-8. Selecting a way to update Windows

Next, you will set up the current date and time, and finally, if your computer has a network card, Windows 7 will prompt you to select your current location (see Figure 1-9; wireless network users will be asked to select a wireless network to connect to). Choose a location that best describes the environment you are in.

That's it! You are now ready to explore Windows 7 (see Figure 1-10).

What's New in Windows 7

The first time you power up Windows 7, you may feel a sense of déjà vu—it looks very similar to Windows Vista. However, behind the familiar UI lies a more powerful and versatile operating system. Subsequent chapters will cover some of the new features in more detail, but here are some of the most prominent new features in Windows 7.

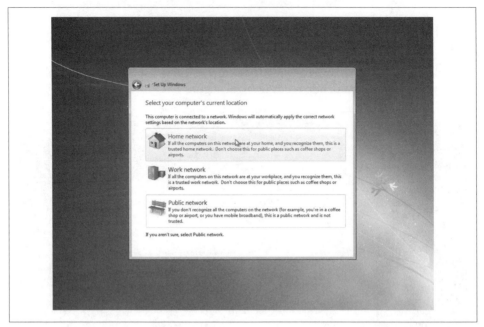

Figure 1-9. Select your computer's current location

Figure 1-10. You are now ready to explore Windows 7

Touchscreen support

Windows 7 is designed with touchscreen support, especially multitouch, in mind. At the time of this writing, companies like Dell and HP were shipping touchscreen computers that work with Windows 7's multitouch. As touchscreen computers are still not common, this book will not discuss the touch capability of Windows 7.

But in case you're interested, to demonstrate the power of touch in Windows 7, Microsoft has created the Microsoft Touch Pack for Windows 7. The Microsoft Touch Pack for Windows 7 is a collection of six applications that are optimized for touch interactions. It consists of three games and three Microsoft Surface (*http://www.micro soft.com/surface/*) applications that have been recreated for Windows 7. These applications are:

Microsoft Surface Globe
  Displays a 3D earth with which you can interact using—what else?—your hands.
Microsoft Surface Collage
  Manages your digital photos; you can resize and rearrange them.
Microsoft Surface Lagoon
  A screensaver that you can interact with through multitouch.
Microsoft Blackboard
  A game utilizing physics where you can use gestures to rotate gears, fans, seesaws, and other objects.
Microsoft Rebound
  A ball game in which you can play against another user or the computer.
Microsoft Garden Pond
  Another interactive game where you use touch to place objects in a virtual pond.

The Microsoft Touch Pack for Windows 7will be made available first to OEMs shipping touch-enabled PCs, although Microsoft may make it available to end users.

New taskbar

Perhaps the most outstanding feature in Windows 7 is the new taskbar. The quick-launch area that most Windows XP and Vista users are so used to is now gone. In place of it is the ability to *pin* your applications icons in the taskbar for easy access, regardless of whether the application is itself running.

Sadly, the classic Start menu has also been disabled in Windows 7. Hopefully, Microsoft will turn it back on in a future service pack, or determined hackers will find a way to replace it.

Figure 1-11 shows the new taskbar in Windows 7 with several application icons in it. On the left is the Start menu button, followed by Internet Explorer 8 (IE8), Windows Explorer, and Windows Media Player.

Figure 1-11. The new taskbar in Windows 7

By default, the taskbar in Windows 7 has three applications pinned to it—IE8, Windows Explorer, and Windows Media Player. As these applications are used often, they are given permanent spots in the taskbar (for more information about pinning, see the section "Pinning Applications to the Taskbar" on page 21). As you can see in Figure 1-11, the Media Player application does not have the rectangular border around it—this signifies that the application is not running currently. Next to the Windows Media Player icon are: Paint, Notepad (also not currently running), and Word.

New Show desktop shortcut

In the taskbar is another button known as the Show desktop shortcut. The Show desktop shortcut is the button on the extreme right of the taskbar (see Figure 1-12).

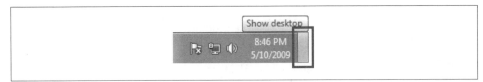

Figure 1-12. The Show desktop shortcut button

Positioning the mouse over this button will make all the current windows transparent (this feature requires an Aero-capable video card and an edition of Windows 7 that supports Aero), revealing the desktop (known as "peeking at the desktop"; see Figure 1-13).

 You can disable the "peeking at the desktop" feature by right-clicking the Show desktop shortcut button and unchecking the Peek at Desktop item.

Clicking this button minimizes all opened windows and shows the desktop.

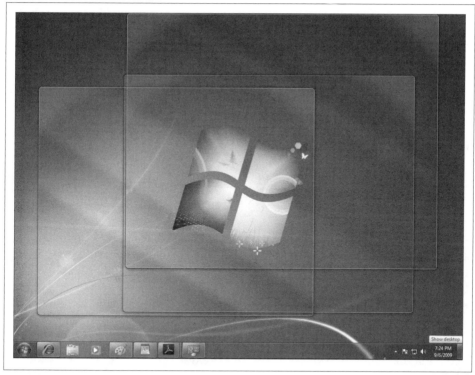

Figure 1-13. Peeking at the desktop in action

Aero Peek, Aero Shake, and Aero Snap

Another cool new feature in Windows 7 is *Aero Peek*. Aero Peek displays live previews of active applications when you move the mouse over the application icon in the taskbar. Figure 1-14 shows Aero Peek in action when the mouse hovers over the IE icon in the taskbar.

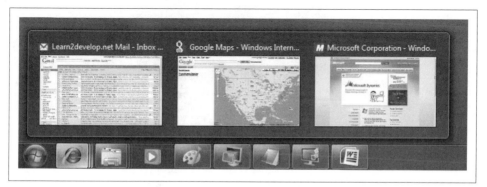

Figure 1-14. Aero Peek in action

Aero Peek requires an Aero-capable video card and a Windows 7 edition that supports Aero. Aero Shake and Aero Snap will work on any Windows 7 system.

Windows displays the live previews of all running instances of IE. When the mouse hovers over one of the live previews, the selected window appears, and the rest of the windows turn transparent. To select the window, simply click the live preview.

 When an application has too many open windows, the title of each window will be displayed in a list instead of live preview thumbnails.

Aero Shake allows users to quickly minimize all nonactive windows by "shaking" the current active window. To see Aero Shake in action, open up a few windows, click the title bar of one window, and use the mouse to "shake" the application. You will notice that all other windows will now be minimized, leaving the current window. To get all the other windows back to their respective states, perform the same shaking action again and they should now all appear again.

Another very useful UI feature in Windows 7 is *Aero Snap*. How many times have you tried to arrange multiple windows on your desktop so that you see the windows side-by-side? In Windows 7, when you drag a window to the left side of the screen, the window is automatically docked onto the left of the screen (see Figure 1-15), occupying half the screen. Likewise, when dragged to the right, the window will be docked to the right. When dragged to the top, the window will be maximized. Besides dragging, Windows 7 provides several shortcuts (see Table 1-1) for window management.

Figure 1-15. Aero Snap works by docking the window to the sides of the screen

Table 1-1. Aero Snap keyboard shortcuts

Shortcuts	Descriptions
Windows Key + ↓	Restores/minimizes window
Windows Key + ←	Docks window to left of screen
Windows Key + →	Docks window to right of screen
Windows Key + ↑	Maximizes window
Windows Key + Shift + ←	Moves to left monitor
Windows Key + Shift + →	Moves to right monitor

Gadgets

Microsoft first introduced gadgets in Vista. *Gadgets* are small utility applications that "float" on your screen, providing quick access to them. In Windows 7, gadgets are not confined to the sidebar (which itself was docked to one side of your screen in Vista) but are free to roam about on your desktop (see Figure 1-16).

Figure 1-16. Gadgets can now roam the entire desktop without restrictions

Revised Paint and WordPad Applications

The venerable Paint and WordPad applications (see Figure 1-17) finally got a revision in Windows 7. This time, both of them were updated to use the new ribbon interface that was introduced in Office 2007.

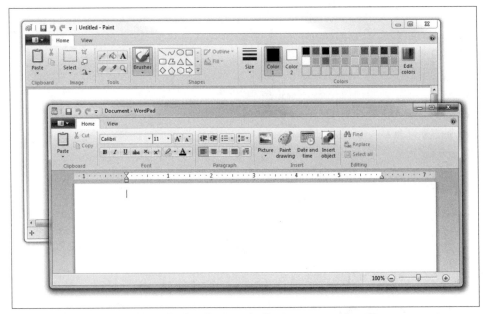

Figure 1-17. The Paint and WordPad applications both sport a new ribbon UI

Calculator

Besides the Paint and WordPad applications, another longtime built-in Windows application has also received some new improvements. The Calculator now has two additional modes (in addition to the Standard and Scientific modes): Programmer and Statistics (see Figure 1-18).

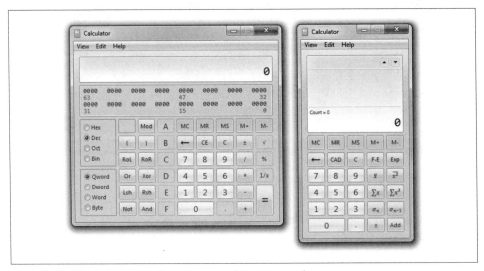

Figure 1-18. The Calculator in Programmer and Statistics modes

Besides the two new modes, the calculator also allows you to perform conversion tasks such as unit and date conversions. It also provides worksheets for you to calculate mortgages, vehicle leases, and fuel economy (see Figure 1-19).

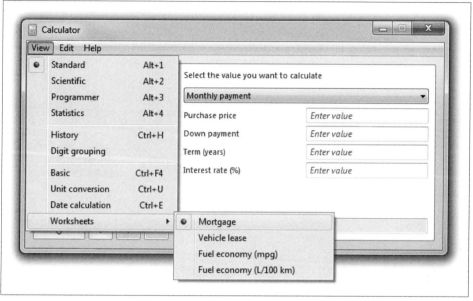

Figure 1-19. The new worksheets in the Windows 7 Calculator

Summary

In this chapter, you have seen the various editions of Windows 7 and the system requirements that you need to satisfy in order to run it. Over the years, Microsoft has streamlined the installation process—and Windows 7 is no exception. Windows 7 performs exceedingly well, and stays out of your way thanks to a less naggy UAC. In the following chapters, you will learn more about each of the new features of Windows 7 and how you can use each of them to your advantage.

CHAPTER 2

Getting Around Windows 7

In Chapter 1, we took a quick glance at the various new features in Windows 7. Among the new features are the much improved taskbar, the improved capabilities of gadgets, and the many UI improvements that make the Windows experience a much more enjoyable one.

In this chapter, we will take a more detailed look at three features that have the most effect on your daily Windows experience:

Taskbar
> The taskbar is now more than just a windows-switcher—it is also an application launcher. You'll learn how mastering the taskbar will make your life easier.

Libraries
> The Libraries is a new feature in Windows 7. Using the Libraries, you can group your files and folders into logical units so they are easier to manage.

Desktop Gadgets
> Gadgets in Windows 7 now have a new lease on life. In Windows Vista, gadgets were constrained to the Sidebar, which was never really a popular feature among people with small-screen computers (netbooks and small portable computers). In Windows 7, gadgets are free to roam about on your desktop.

Taskbar

One of the most significant changes in Windows 7 is the taskbar. The new taskbar in Windows 7 combines the good old Windows taskbar with the Quick Launch feature available in previous versions of Windows. As mentioned, it is no longer just a windows switcher—it is also an application launcher, in which application icons can be pinned for easy access.

Aero Peek

In Windows 7, mousing over an icon in the taskbar whose application is running reveals the live thumbnails of all the opened windows of that application. For example, Figure 2-1 shows the live thumbnails of all the IE windows currently open when the mouse is moved over the IE icon. If your computer or Windows edition is not Aero-capable (or if you've chosen a non-Aero theme), you will instead see a list of open window titles.

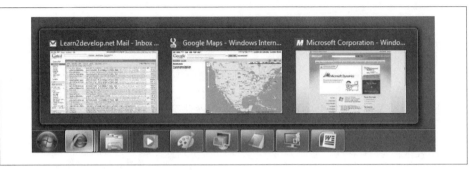

Figure 2-1. Aero Peek displays live thumbnails of all opened windows

As you move the mouse over the live thumbnails of the IE windows, the corresponding window will appear on the screen (see Figure 2-2) and all other windows will turn transparent, allowing you to quickly preview the content of the current window. If you decide to switch to the selected window, simply click the thumbnail, and the selected window will now be active.

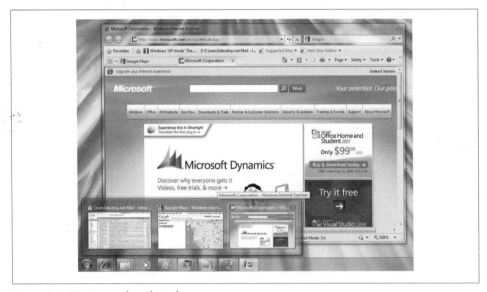

Figure 2-2. Viewing a selected window

For most applications, each open window is represented by a single thumbnail. For IE, however, each tab page or window is represented by a single thumbnail. Developers writing applications for the Windows 7 platform have the flexibility to decide how their applications are represented by Aero Peek in the taskbar.

Pinning Applications to the Taskbar

In the previous versions of Windows, only running applications appear in the taskbar. In Windows 7, you can keep an application's icon in the taskbar even when it's not running.

This feature is very similar to that of Dock for Mac OS X, where frequently used applications can have their icons "docked" on the Dock.

Applications can have their icons "pinned" in the taskbar permanently. For example, Windows Media Player (see Figure 2-3) is pinned by default to the taskbar, as it is a commonly used utility application. Clicking the icon will open the Windows Media Player.

Figure 2-3. The Windows Media Player is pinned to the taskbar by default

You can unpin a pinned application icon from the taskbar by right-clicking it and then selecting "Unpin this program from taskbar."

So, how do you know which applications are currently running and which ones are merely pinned to the taskbar? The taskbar highlights all running applications with a rectangular border (see Figure 2-4); those not running do not have any border. Applications that require attention have flashing icons (see the rightmost icon in Figure 2-4).

Figure 2-4. The taskbar uses a rectangular border to denote running applications; flashing icons indicate a call for attention

Jump Lists

When you right-click an application icon in the taskbar, Windows 7 will display a list of menus known as *Jump Lists*. Jump Lists contain several default options as well as a list of *tasks* and *destinations* that you can perform within the selected application. For example, Figure 2-5 shows the Jump List of the Control Panel application. It contains a section called Recent that displays a list of recently used applications in the Control Panel.

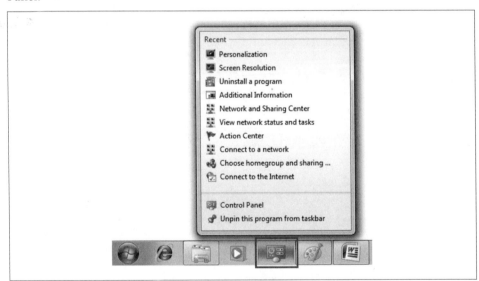

Figure 2-5. The taskbar showing the list of recent activities performed with the Control Panel application

The Jump List of an application can also be seen in the Start menu. If you click the Start menu, you will notice that there are several items with an arrow next to them. For example, clicking the Control Panel item (see Figure 2-6) will reveal its Jump Lists.

Figure 2-6. Jump Lists can also be seen in the Start menu

Tasks

As mentioned, Jump Lists contain a list of tasks and destinations. The *tasks* list contains application-specific actions that you can perform with an application. Tasks are context-free actions, independent of whether the application is running. As an example, the Jump List for Internet Explorer (see Figure 2-7) contains a Tasks section in which you can invoke InPrivate Browsing or create a New Tab page.

Destinations

Besides showing the recent tasks that you have performed with an application, the Jump Lists of an application also shows the *destinations* of an application. For example, in

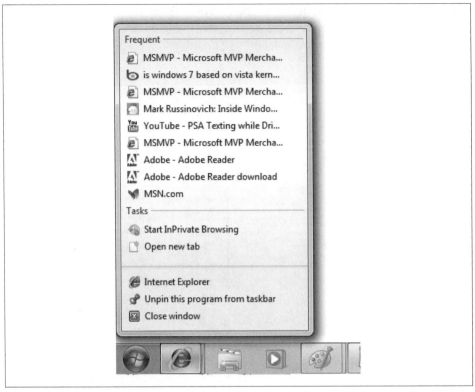

Figure 2-7. The Frequent destination shows the list of frequently visited sites

the Jump List of Internet Explorer (as shown in Figure 2-7), you will see a section called Frequent, which displays the list of frequently visited websites (the destinations of a web browser).

The Difference Between Tasks and Destinations

The easiest way to differentiate tasks from destinations is to think of a task as a verb and a destination as a noun. For instance, some examples of tasks are:

- Play all music (Windows Media Player)
- Resume previous list (Windows Media Player)
- Go to MSN home page (Live Messenger)
- New Note (Sticky Notes)

Some examples of destinations are:

- Recently visited websites (Internet Explorer)
- Documents (Word)
- Images (Paint)

Default entries

By default, a Jump List has at least two list items in it. Figure 2-8 shows the Jump List for the Paint application. The first item allows you to launch a new instance of the application. The second allows you to pin (or unpin if it has already been pinned onto the taskbar) the program from the taskbar.

Figure 2-8. The default items in a Jump List

The third item closes the application and will appear only if at least one instance of the program is already running.

To pin an application onto the taskbar, first launch the application, and then right-click the application's icon in the taskbar. Select the "Pin this program to taskbar" list item. By doing so, the application will now always appear in the taskbar.

You can also pin items listed in the Recent destination. For example, Figure 2-9 shows the Recent destination of the Jump List for Word. You can pin an item by clicking the pin icon shown to the right of the item. The pinned item will then appear in the Pinned destination.

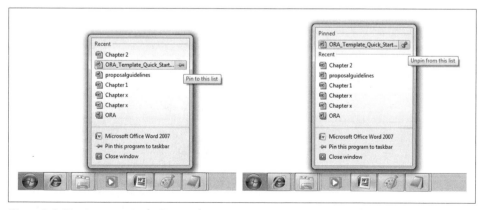

Figure 2-9. Pinning items in the Recent destination

Some applications, such as Internet Explorer 8, let you pin destinations by dragging them to the application's taskbar icon. To pin a web page to IE8's Jump List, drag the web page icon to IE8's taskbar icon. The web page icon appears to the left of its URL in the location field at the top of the IE8 window.

Libraries

In Windows XP and Windows Vista, you have special folders named "My Documents," "My Pictures," and so on for storing your files. However, not many people actively used these folders for storing their personal data. Instead, people created their own folders, with names like *C:\My project June 2008* and *C:\photos\Photos from Japan trip 2007*. Although there is nothing wrong with this approach, it makes indexing and searching very time-consuming, not to mention frustrating.

In Windows 7, Microsoft has attempted to address this problem with the concept of *Libraries*. Conceptually, Libraries are a central repository of all the various folders on your computer. To search for files in your computer, go to the Libraries and navigate the various subfolders contained within it. You can still create an assortment of folders, but you can avoid the chaos by adding a folder to one of your libraries.

Exploring Libraries

The Libraries are found in Windows Explorer. Figure 2-10 shows the application with its four default libraries—*Documents*, *Music*, *Pictures*, and *Videos*.

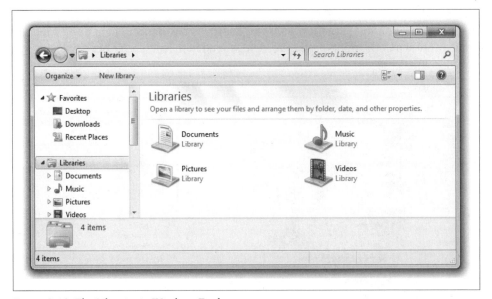

Figure 2-10. The Libraries in Windows Explorer

When you click the arrow to the left of the *Documents* library (or double-click its icon), you will observe that there are two folders contained within it (see Figure 2-11): *My Documents* and *Public Documents*. These two folders are actual folders located elsewhere on your computer.

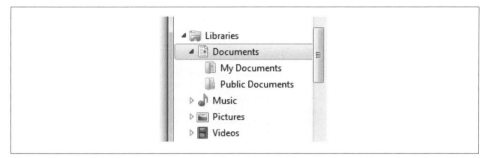

Figure 2-11. The Documents library, which contains two folders

 Each library is mapped to two separate folders for a good reason. The first folder, called the *private* folder, is for saving your own personal data. The second folder, called the *public* folder, is for everyone. If you use the HomeGroup feature (see Chapter 3) to share files, the private folder will have read-only permission. This means that other users on the network can view what is in your private folder, but cannot make changes to it. In contrast, public folders will have read-and-write permissions, which means that other users can view their content as well as make changes to it.

In fact, *My Documents* is mapped to *C:\Users\username\My Documents* and *Public Documents* is mapped to *C:\Users\Public\Public Documents*.

With the Libraries, all your content should ideally be grouped under the default libraries. For example, all your documents should be saved in either the *My Documents* or *Public Documents* folder. When you need to search for documents, you simply go to the *Documents* library and start your search from there.

Creating Your Own Library

Of course, not everyone wants to save their documents in a generic folder named *My Documents*. You can still save your documents in a specific folder—say, *C:\My Report June 2009*—and then link it with the Libraries. Suppose you want to create a library to contain all your reports. In this case, the first thing you do is to create a new library by right-clicking Libraries and selecting New→Library (see Figure 2-12).

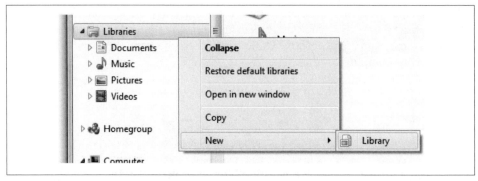

Figure 2-12. Creating a new library

Name your library (for this example, I have named it as *Reports*) and your newly created library will now be empty (see Figure 2-13).

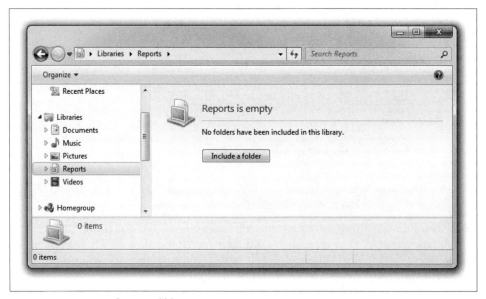

Figure 2-13. Your newly created library

To link your library to an actual folder, click the "Include a folder" button and specify a folder name. For example, I have added the *C:\My Report June 2009* folder to my library. The *Reports* library now looks like Figure 2-14.

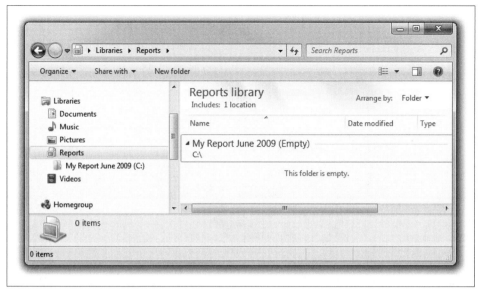

Figure 2-14. Adding a folder to a library

To add more folders to the library, click the "1 location" link (see Figure 2-15).

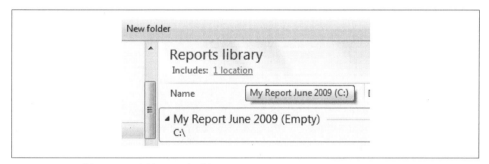

Figure 2-15. Adding more folders to the library

Click the Add button to specify a folder to add to the library (see Figure 2-16). You can add as many folders are you like.

Figure 2-16. Adding additional folders to the library

Note that the first folder added to the library will be the *default save location* for the library. This means that when you drag-and-drop an item to the *Reports* library, the item will be copied into the *My Report June 2009* folder (because this is the first folder added to the library).

You specify another folder as the default save location by right-clicking a folder in this list and choosing "Set as default save location." You can change the order in which these appear by right-clicking and choosing Move Up or Move Down.

You can now use the library just like a normal folder. The files inside each folder are saved in their respective directories, but the library itself offers a logical grouping of related files (see Figure 2-17).

Figure 2-17. Using the library

 You may remove the entire library if you want, but this will not remove the files or directories that are part of the library.

Desktop Gadgets

In Windows 7, Microsoft eliminated the Windows Sidebar, because feedback showed that docking gadgets to the side of the screen is very restrictive, especially for small-screen portable computer users.

What Is the Windows Sidebar?

Windows Vista included a feature called the Windows Sidebar. The Sidebar is a rectangular strip displayed on the side of your screen (hence the name "sidebar") that hosts mini-applications known as *gadgets*. A Sidebar gadget is an easy-to-use mini-application that is designed to provide information at a glance. Sidebar gadgets afford an easy way to access information at your fingertips and can be easily created by developers familiar with HTML and scripting languages like JavaScript.

In Windows 7, you can now display the gadgets directly on the desktop rather than be constrained to the Sidebar.

 Windows 7 desktop gadgets are fully compatible with the Sidebar gadgets in Windows Vista.

To view the list of gadgets installed on your computer, right-click the desktop and select Gadgets. A list of gadgets will be shown (see Figure 2-18).

Figure 2-18. Displaying the list of available gadgets

As shown in Figure 2-18, Windows 7 includes 10 default gadgets. To add a gadget to your desktop, double-click the gadget. By default, the gadget will be docked to the right side of the screen. Figure 2-19 shows the Slide Show gadget. Unlike in Windows Vista, you can now drag the gadget onto any part of the desktop.

Figure 2-19. The Slide Show gadget, docked to the right side of the screen

To locate more gadgets, click the "Get more gadgets online" link. You will be shown a page displaying a list of gadgets that you can add (see Figure 2-20).

Figure 2-20. Viewing the list of gadgets you can download

To download a gadget, click the "Download gadget" link below each gadget. You will be prompted to open or save the gadget. Click Open (see Figure 2-21) to directly download and install the gadget.

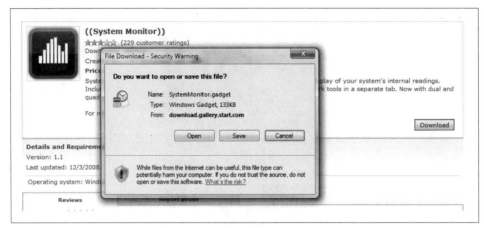

Figure 2-21. Downloading a gadget

Once the download is complete, IE will prompt you with a security warning to ask whether you want to run the application. Click Run to open the gadget. Next, you will be prompted with another security warning. Click Install to install the gadget on your computer.

Once the installation is complete, you will see the new gadget in the Gadgets window (see Figure 2-22), and it will also automatically add a copy of itself to your desktop.

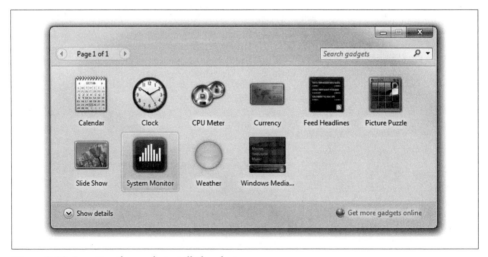

Figure 2-22. Locating the newly installed gadget

Summary

In this chapter, you learned about the improvements made to the taskbar. The new Aero Peek feature allows you to preview windows without switching to them. And Jump Lists allow you to jump to a specific destination or task by simply right-clicking an application icon. In addition, you also learned about the new Libraries feature, which makes it easy for you to organize your files. And in Windows 7, the Desktop Gadgets has a new lease on life.

In the next chapter, you will learn more about another new feature in Windows 7: *HomeGroup*. HomeGroup will make use of the new Libraries feature to allow you to easily share files with other users on the same network.

CHAPTER 3

File Sharing

File Sharing has been one of the features common to all Windows operating systems. Besides sharing files with other Windows computers, the File Sharing feature in Windows also allows users to share files with other non-Windows computers, such as Mac OS X and Linux users. In Windows 7, file sharing has been further simplified with the new HomeGroup feature.

In this chapter, you will learn about the new HomeGroup feature, as well as learn how to share files with other computers on your network.

HomeGroup

One of the challenges with previous versions of Windows is how to share files easily with other users on the network. Suppose that you have multiple files on your notebook computer that you have created while you were in the office and when you go back home you want to use the files on your home desktop computer. Prior to Windows 7, you had to create a shared folder on your notebook, navigate to the Network Neighborhood on the other computer, and look for the notebook's shared folder.

In Windows 7, Microsoft has made file sharing very simple with HomeGroup. Using HomeGroup, you can easily share files as well as your digital media (such as music and videos) with other users on the same network. What's more, HomeGroup also allows you to share one or more USB printers connected to a single computer with the rest of the users on the network.

Wireless Networking

Connecting to wireless networks is now very simple in Windows 7. As in the previous versions of Windows, there is the wireless signal icon in the system tray. However, unlike previous versions, you can now click the wireless icon to display a list of wireless networks available (see Figure 3-1).

To connect to a wireless network, simply move the mouse over the network name and click the Connect button. If the wireless network requires a key, you will be prompted to enter one. And you are connected!

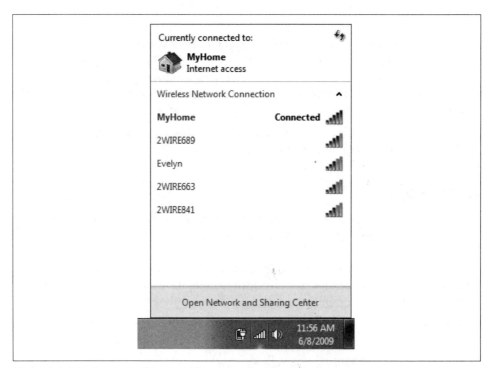

Figure 3-1. Selecting from a list of wireless networks

HomeGroup revolves around the concept of a "home" network. When you are at home, you want to be able to share files and printers easily with other family members. Hence, the HomeGroup feature will work only if you are connected to the Home network (see Figure 3-2).

When you are connected to the Home network, Windows 7 will initiate a network discovery to start looking for other computers on the same network and will check to see whether a HomeGroup is available for joining.

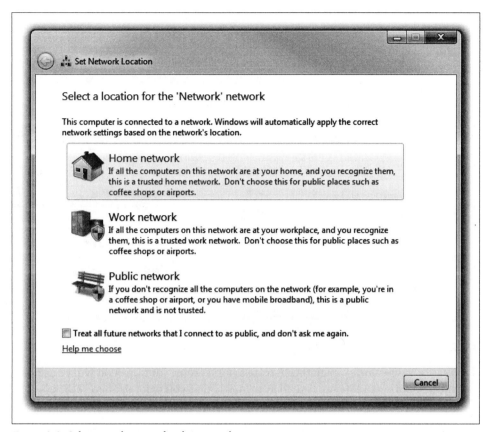

Figure 3-2. Selecting a location for the network

You can easily switch to another network by going to Control Panel→Network and Sharing Center and clicking the link below the Network name (it will be labeled Home network, Work network, or Public network).

Creating a New HomeGroup

Creating a HomeGroup is straightforward. Go to Control Panel and click "Choose homegroup and sharing options," which is found under the Network and Internet section. If there is currently no HomeGroup created in your Home network, you will see the screen as shown in Figure 3-3.

Windows 7 Starter Edition cannot create a HomeGroup, but it can join a HomeGroup that you've created on another computer. Any users on the Home network can create a HomeGroup. As soon as one user has created a HomeGroup, the rest can just join the HomeGroup.

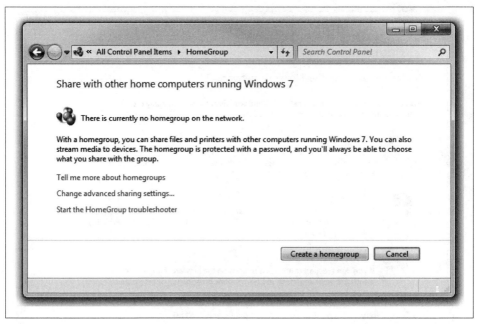

Figure 3-3. Creating a new HomeGroup

To create a HomeGroup, click the "Create a homegroup" button. You will be asked to select the libraries and devices (such as printers) that you want to share. Click Next.

Only the default libraries created by Windows are displayed for you to select. To share your own custom libraries, refer to the next section.

A password will be generated. Users who want to participate in this HomeGroup will need this password. Click Finish to complete the creation process.

Changing the HomeGroup Password

You can always change the password that HomeGroup has generated for you. However, Microsoft's research has shown that users normally use their own personal password for this purpose, and when they realize that this password must be shared with those who need to join the HomeGroup, they are generally reluctant to share the password. Hence, it is usually a good idea to use the generated password.

If you want to change the password, click the "Change the password..." link as shown in Figure 3-4.

The HomeGroup window should now look like Figure 3-4.

Figure 3-4. The HomeGroup window, showing the various options available

To leave the HomeGroup, click the "Leave the homegroup…" link.

Controlling what is shared (and what is not)

In Chapter 2, you learned about the new Libraries feature in Windows 7. Recall that for each of the default libraries (*Documents*, *Music*, *Pictures*, and *Videos*), there are two locations. For example, the *Documents* library has two locations: *My Documents* and *Public Documents* (see Figure 3-5).

By default, when you share a library, Windows 7 will apply different security settings for each of the locations in the four libraries. The first folder (for example, *My Pictures*) will have read-only permission applied to it. This means that users in your HomeGroup can only view the items in the folder, but not make changes to it. The other folder (for example, *Public Pictures*) will have read-and-write permission.

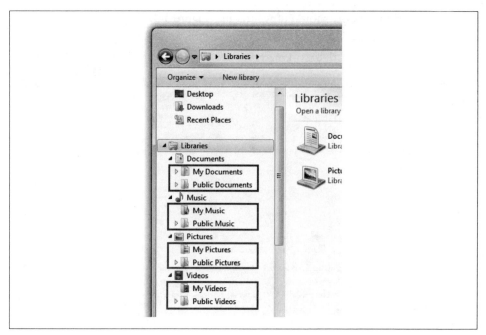

Figure 3-5. Each library has two locations

To change the share permission of a library, select the library, click the "Share with" button, and select the relevant permission: *Nobody*, *HomeGroup (Read)*, or *HomeGroup (Read/Write)*; see Figure 3-6.

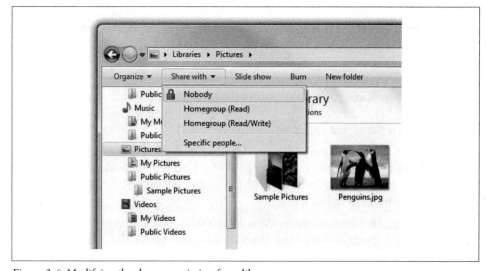

Figure 3-6. Modifying the share permission for a library

You can also share a library with specific people by selecting the "Specific people..." menu item.

You can also modify each libraries' location's share permission by selecting the location and then choosing the "Share with" button. In addition, you can also use this technique to share your own custom library.

Joining a HomeGroup

Once a HomeGroup is created, users on the same Home network can join the HomeGroup and share files and devices (such as printers). If someone in the Home network has created a HomeGroup, the HomeGroup window will appear.

Windows 7 will also try to detect an available HomeGroup during installation time. If there is one, you will be invited to join the group.

To join the HomeGroup, click the "Join now" button. You will be asked to select the libraries and devices that you want to share. Click Next to continue.

You will then be asked to enter the password to join the network. Enter the password, click Next, and then click Finish to join the HomeGroup.

Sharing Files

Once you have joined a HomeGroup, you will be able to view the files shared by other users in the HomeGroup. To view the files, open Windows Explorer and look for the item named HomeGroup displayed on the left side of the window (see Figure 3-7).

When you click a shared library (such as the *Music* library shown in Figure 3-7), Windows Explorer will display all the files inside the two locations on the right side of the window (*My Music* and *Public Music*). If you drag-and-drop files into a library, the files will automatically be copied onto the public folder. This makes sense, as the public folder has read-and-write permissions.

Sharing Printers

One really cool feature of the HomeGroup is the ability to share printers. Very often, you have a printer connected to a computer via USB and you might want to share it with other computers in your home network. Prior to Windows 7, sharing printers required you to perform a series of steps to configure the printers for sharing.

Figure 3-7. Viewing files shared by other users in the HomeGroup

In Windows 7, you can share a printer easily using the HomeGroup feature. When another computer joins the HomeGroup, it will be able see the printer connected to your computer. If the printer has the Windows logo, HomeGroup users will instantly see the printer in their Devices and Printers window. Figure 3-8 shows the printer connected to a computer on the HomeGroup made available to the local computer.

> The Windows logo indicates that the printer manufacturer is participating in a program that ensures it is safe to automatically install its driver on your computer without your direct consent.

If the printer does not have the Windows logo, the HomeGroup page will display a message indicating that it has found a shared printer on the home network (see Figure 3-9). Click the "Install printer" button to install the printer driver.

Figure 3-8. Printers shared from another computer

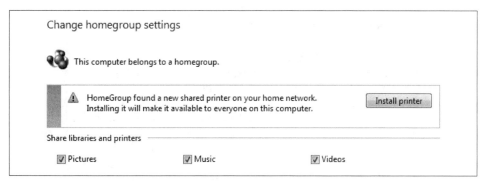

Figure 3-9. Detecting a shared printer on the home network

You will be prompted to install the driver for the printer. Click "Install driver."

The best part of this is that the installation of the driver is automatic—the driver is copied from the host computer (connected to the printer) and installed on the local computer. With HomeGroup, a printer attached to one computer is made available to everyone in the HomeGroup.

 If you are logged in as a normal user, installing the printer driver will require an administrator's credentials.

Streaming Music

Using the new HomeGroup feature, you can now stream music from one Windows 7 computer to other computers and devices.

To stream your music and videos to other devices on the home network, check the "Stream my pictures, music, and videos to all devices on my home network" checkbox in the HomeGroup window.

To customize the files streamed to each individual computer in the HomeGroup, click the "Choose media streaming options..." link. The Media streaming options window will now appear (see Figure 3-10).

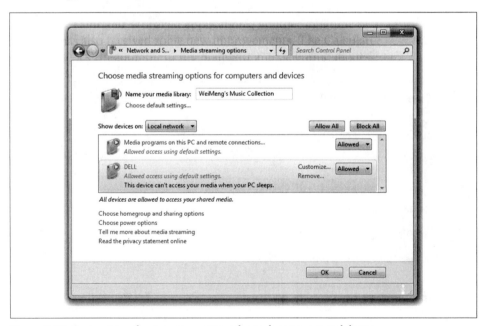

Figure 3-10. Customizing the streaming options for each computer and device

You can give a name to your media library and then click the Customize... link for each device on your network to control which files to stream to each device.

Users on the HomeGroup will now be able to see your music collection from within Media Player (see Figure 3-11).

Figure 3-11. Viewing the shared music collections from Windows Media Player

The shared music collection is also available in the Windows Media Center.

File Sharing with Windows XP

Though the new HomeGroup feature in Windows 7 makes file sharing very simple, it is incompatible with previous versions of Windows. If you need to share files with Windows XP or Windows Vista computers, you have to rely on the old trusty file-sharing mechanism:

1. To share files with other users and computers on the network, turn off password-protected sharing so that users can access the files without authentication.

2. Go to Control Panel→Network and Internet→Network and Sharing Center. Click the "Change advanced sharing settings" link.

3. Scroll to the bottom of the page and locate the "Password protected sharing" section (see Figure 3-12). Turn off the password-protected sharing, as this will allow other users to access your shared file without needing an account on your computer. Click the "Save changes" button when done.

 The previous step is needed only if you want everyone on your network to access your files. If you want to share only with specific users on other computers, you will need to create an account and password for them on your computer so that they can use it to access your files.

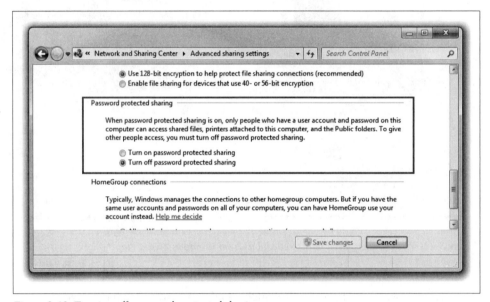

Figure 3-12. Turning off password-protected sharing

4. Create a folder that you want to share. For example, create a folder on the desktop and name it *Common Files*.

5. Right-click the folder and select Properties.

6. Click the Sharing tab and click the Share… button. You will see the File Sharing window, as shown in Figure 3-13.

 Alternatively, you can also use the new "Share with" button located in Windows Explorer to configure file sharing.

7. Click the drop-down arrow to select from a list of users who can access the shared folder. Once selected, click Add to add the user to the shared list. You can also configure the read/write permission for each user. Here, I am sharing the files with everyone on the network.

8. Click Share.

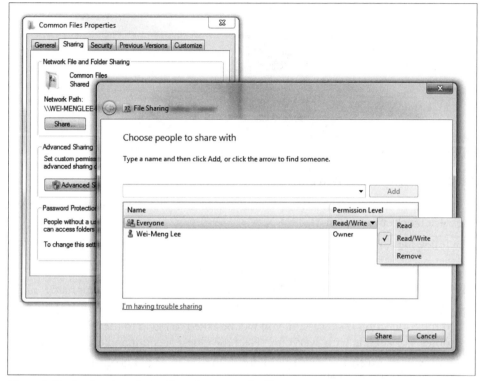

Figure 3-13. Configuring who is allowed to access the file

On the Windows XP computer, open the My Network Places window, and you should be able to see the various shared folders on the network. Double-click the one that contains your shared folder.

You will now be able to access the content in the shared folder.

Viewing Shared Folders from Within Windows 7

In Windows 7, to view shared folders from other computers, launch Windows Explorer and expand the Network item on the bottom-left corner of the window (see Figure 3-14). All shared folders on the network will be listed here.

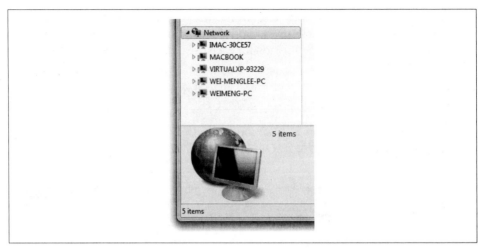

Figure 3-14. Viewing the various shared folders on the network in Windows 7

File Sharing with Mac OS X

If you want to share your Windows 7 files with Mac OS X users, use the SMB (Server Message Block) protocol in Mac OS X.

The following steps outline how you can view shared folders in Mac OS X:

1. In Finder, select Go→Connect to Server....

2. Specify the "smb://" prefix, followed by the IP address (or computer name) of the Windows 7 computer and the ":139" port number. Click Connect.

3. If the connection is successful, you will be asked to log in to the Windows 7 computer. For sharing with everyone, select the Guest account and click Connect.

4. You will be asked to select the folder to mount in Mac OS X (see Figure 3-15). Select the folder and click OK.

5. Finally, the shared folder is now available in Mac OS X.

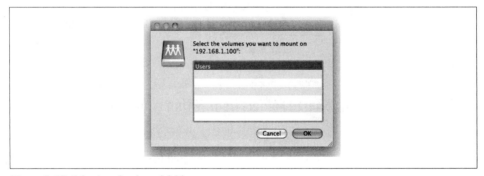

Figure 3-15. Selecting the shared folder to mount

Summary

In Windows 7, Microsoft greatly simplified file- and printer-sharing using the new HomeGroup feature. Using HomeGroup, sharing files and printers is now a seamless experience for Windows users. Not only that, but the ability to stream music from one Windows 7 computer to another also makes Windows 7 an ideal platform on which to build your next media center.

Although HomeGroup works only on Windows 7 computers, file sharing with other platforms (such as Mac OS X, Windows XP, and Windows Vista) can still be performed using the old file-sharing mechanism.

CHAPTER 4

Security

On the security front, Windows 7 has streamlined several features found in Windows Vista, making them much more accessible and less irritating in this new version of Windows. For example, the infamous User Account Control (UAC) is one of the most annoying features in Vista. In this version of Windows, Microsoft has tweaked UAC so that it interrupts users only when needed. Microsoft has also replaced the Security Center in Vista with the new Action Center in Windows 7, which focuses not just on displaying problems, but also on offering suggestions and solutions to solve problems. The Credential Manager now has the ability to back up its credential information to a file. In addition, Enterprise and Ultimate users can now encrypt a portable thumb drive using BitLocker To Go.

Action Center

In Windows 7, Microsoft has designated the new Action Center as the one-stop place to find all your system maintenance and security messages. The key design goal of the Action Center is to help users solve system issues quickly and conveniently.

The system tray is now less cluttered, compared with its appearance in previous versions of Windows—it now has four main icons: Action Center, Network, Speaker volume, and Date and Time (see Figure 4-1). Mobile computers will have a power icon as well.

Figure 4-1. The four icons in the System tray

In particular, the Action Center icon (represented as a white flag, which will include a red "x" if there are important messages requiring your attention) replaces several notification icons from Vista, reducing much clutter. When you click the Action Center icon, a pop-up window displays a summary of system messages of varying importance levels. In addition, it also provides a way for you to resolve the error. For example, Figure 4-2 shows that I have two messages for my computer—one important and one normal. The pop up also includes two links for me to resolve my problems—one to find an antivirus program and one to set up a backup for my computer. To view the messages, click the message icons or click the Open Action Center link.

Figure 4-2. Viewing the messages summary and remedy links for the Action Center icon

The Action Center will display the details of the messages along with a button to help you solve the issue.

Besides displaying messages on maintenance and security-related issues, the Action Center can also help you troubleshoot problems with your computer and restore your computer to its setup from an earlier time.

Messages are classified into two main categories: Security and Maintenance. Security messages relate to issues concerned with:

- Windows Update
- Internet security settings
- Network firewall
- Spyware and related protection
- User Account Control
- Virus protection

Maintenance messages relate to issues concerned with:

- Windows Backup
- Windows Troubleshooting

Messages can be important or normal. Important messages display notification balloons (see Figure 4-3) in the System tray in addition to appearing in Action Center. A good example of an important message balloon is what happens when the Windows Firewall is turned off.

Figure 4-3. Important messages displaying notification balloons

In the Action Center, you can also expand on each message category to view the status of each Security- and Maintenance-related item for your computer.

 The Action Center is for displaying messages and resolving problems, not managing tasks. For example, you can use the Action Center to help you find an antivirus program, but you cannot manage your Windows Firewall in the Action Center.

You have the option to prevent messages from displaying by clicking the Change Action Center settings link in the left side of the Action Center window. Uncheck the item(s) for which you do not want to view a message.

Turning Off Action Center

If you do not want to see the Action Center in the System tray at all, you can turn it off. Perform the following steps to turn Action Center off:

- Right-click the "Show hidden icons" button in the Notification Area (see Figure 4-4) and select "Customize notification icons."
- Click the "Turn system icons on and off" link (see Figure 4-5).
- For the Action Center icon, select Off (see Figure 4-6).

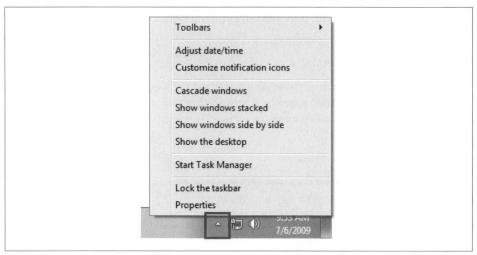

Figure 4-4. Configuring Action Center via the "Show hidden icons" button

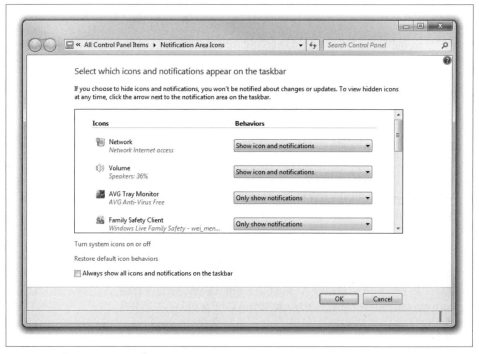

Figure 4-5. Customizing notification area icons

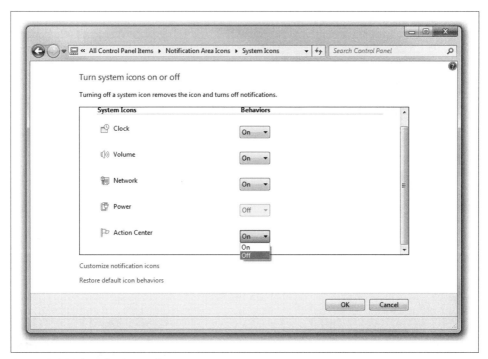

Figure 4-6. Hiding the Action Center

User Account Control

One of the most fiercely criticized features of Windows Vista is the User Account Control (UAC). Whenever a system-level change is made, Vista's UAC displays a dialog box prompting the user to continue or stop. This happens regardless of whether it is a program that is making the changes or the user herself (even though she might be logged in as an administrator). And with the frequency that the UAC displays prompts, most users find it a nuisance rather than a useful security alert feature. Moreover, when the user ends up with too many UAC prompts, it actually defeats the purpose, as users simply give their permission without reading the prompts.

In Windows Vista, Microsoft only provided two options to control UAC—turn it on or turn it off. In Windows 7, Microsoft has fine-tuned the UAC so that you can choose when to be notified if changes happen.

To configure UAC, go to Control Panel and select User Accounts and Family Safety, and then select User Accounts. Click the Change User Account Control settings link.

Notice that you now have four levels to specify how you are notified when changes are made to your computer (see Figure 4-7).

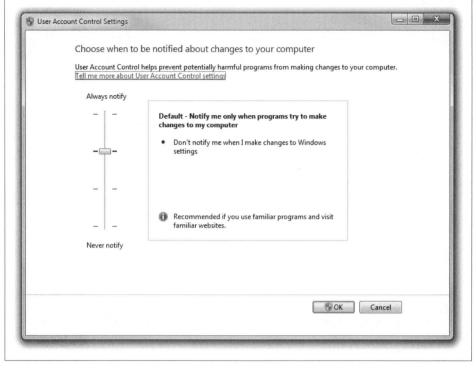

Figure 4-7. Modifying the notification levels of UAC

The four levels are:

- Always notify when programs install software or users make changes to the computer. This is the most naggy option, as all changes require the permission of the user (this is the option used by Vista).
- Notify only when programs make changes to the system. When the user makes changes to the Windows settings, there will be no prompting. This is the default level selected by Windows.
- Notify only when programs make changes to the system without desktop dimming. When the user makes changes to the Windows settings, there will be no prompting.
- The user is never notified. This option is not recommended.

When you select a particular notification level and click OK, you will be prompted to confirm the selection.

The Credential Manager

Windows 7 includes a feature known as the Credential Manager to help users save their credentials to a vault. Although this is not a new feature, in this version it has the ability to back up and restore the vault. In the Credential Manager, all the credentials are stored in a secure location known as the Windows Vault.

To use the Credential Manager, go to Control Panel→User Accounts and Family Safety→Credential Manager. There are three types of credentials you can store using Credential Manager (see Figure 4-8):

Windows credentials
    Stores the credentials of resources such as servers, printers, and the like.

Certificate-based credentials
    Stores certificate-based credentials, such as those from a smartcard.

Generic credentials
    Stores generic credentials, such as online IDs.

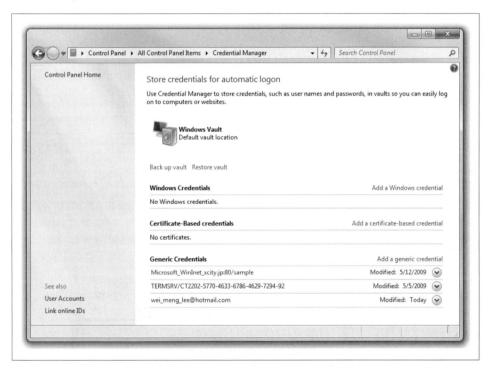

Figure 4-8. Launching the Credential Manager in the Control Panel

Using the Credential Manager

Note that the Credential Manager is designed to work with resources (such as servers and websites) that make use of the Credential Manager API to retrieve the username and password from the Credential Manager. A good example is Windows Live Hotmail.

When you first log in to Windows Live Hotmail, you have an option to save the password to your computer. When you check the "Remember my password" link (see Figure 4-9), the credential (Windows Live ID and password, in this case) is automatically saved into the Credential Manager (see Figure 4-10).

Figure 4-9. Remembering the password on the local computer

Figure 4-10. The credential for Hotmail is saved in the Credential Manager

---

For websites that do not use Windows Live Login, Internet Explorer will store the ID and password pair in the Registry.

If you log out from Hotmail now and try to log in again, you will see that your Windows Live ID is now displayed on the login page and that you can log in automatically (without needing to enter the password) by clicking the "Sign in" button (see Figure 4-11).

Figure 4-11. Logging in automatically

Linking Online IDs

In the previous section, you saw how Hotmail automatically signs you in using the credentials saved in the Credential Manager. The Credential Manager also allows you to link your login user account with an online ID explicitly (such as those given by your email service provider) so that you can sign in to these services automatically. This is done via *online ID providers*. An online ID provider associates your Windows login with an online ID so that when you access your online service you do not need to supply your username and password again.

To manually link your user account with an online ID, click the "Link online IDs" link at the bottom of the Credential Manager window (see Figure 4-12).

Click the "Add an online ID provider" link to locate an online ID provider (see Figure 4-13).

You will be brought to a web page where you can locate an online ID provider. At this moment, only one online ID provider is available—Windows Live. Click the Windows Live icon.

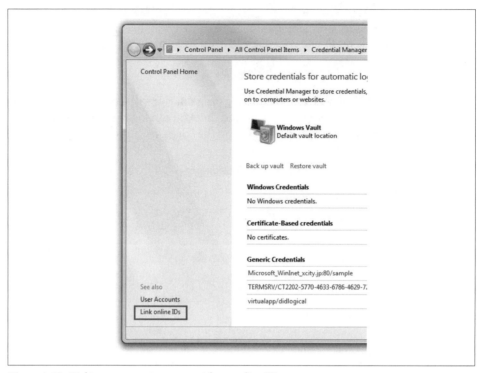

Figure 4-12. Linking your user account with an online ID

Figure 4-13. Adding an online ID provider

You will be brought to a page where you can download the necessary program. In this case, you need to download the Windows Live ID Sign-in Assistant.

Once the download is complete, proceed with the installation. Figure 4-14 shows that the WindowsLiveID provider installed in the Credentials Manager.

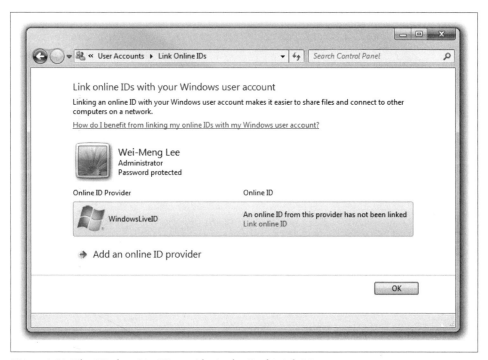

Figure 4-14. The WindowsLiveID provider in the Credentials Manager

Click the "Link online ID" link to add an online ID. Enter your Live ID.

You should now see the credentials you entered (see Figure 4-15).

Now when you use any of the Windows Live services (such as Hotmail and Messenger), you will see that your credentials are automatically filled in for you.

Backing Up the Credentials

A new feature of the Credential Manager in Windows 7 is its ability to back up your credentials to the filesystem. To back up the vault, click the "Back up vault" link.

You will be asked to select a path to back up the vault. Click the Browse... button and specify the path and name of the backup vault. Click Next.

To continue, press Ctrl-Alt-Delete. You will now be asked to protect the file with a password. Enter the password twice and the vault will be backed up.

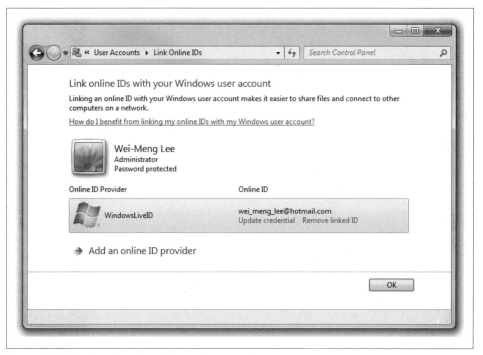

Figure 4-15. Viewing the credentials you just entered

 It is recommended that you save the backup vault to external storage.

To restore the vault, click the "Restore vault" link and supply the password used to protect the file.

BitLocker Drive Encryption

In Windows Vista, you had the BitLocker Drive Encryption feature that allowed you to encrypt the content of entire volumes. In Windows 7, Microsoft has extended this feature to include removable hard disks and thumb drives. This new feature is known as BitLocker To Go.

 The encryption performed by BitLocker is transparent to the user—you will use the drive normally and Windows 7 will automatically encrypt the data on the fly when you write to the drive. Likewise, Windows will decrypt the data on the fly when you read from the drive.

BitLocker

The BitLocker Drive Encryption feature in Windows 7 (also available in Windows Vista) allows you to encrypt your hard drives so that it is safe from unauthorized access. Using BitLocker, all data written to a hard drive stays encrypted when it is stored on the drive. When the OS reads the data, it is automatically decrypted. However, if a BitLocker-encrypted drive is removed from a computer, its content will not be accessible unless the correct password is provided. This way, BitLocker helps protect the integrity and security of your data.

Unlike the Encrypting File System (EFS), which allows you to selectively encrypt files, BitLocker encrypts the entire drive.

There are two types of hard drives you can encrypt using BitLocker:

Operating system drive
This is the drive where Windows 7 is installed in.

Data drive(s)
This includes internal data drives attached to your computer.

BitLocker is available only in the Enterprise and Ultimate editions of Windows 7.

To encrypt the operating system drive using BitLocker, right-click the C: drive and select "Turn on BitLocker..." (see Figure 4-16).

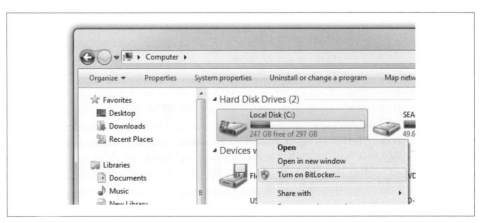

Figure 4-16. Encrypting the C: drive using BitLocker

Alternatively, you can manage BitLocker on all your drives via the BitLocker Drive Encryption application (see Figure 4-17) in the Control Panel.

In order to use BitLocker to encrypt your hard drive containing your operating system, your computer needs to have the Trusted Platform Module (TPM) chip. BitLocker uses the TPM chip to store the keys that are used to decrypt your encrypted drive during bootup time. Alternatively, if your computer does not have the TPM chip, you can store the encryption key on a USB thumb drive. In this case, you need to insert your USB drive into your computer during bootup time.

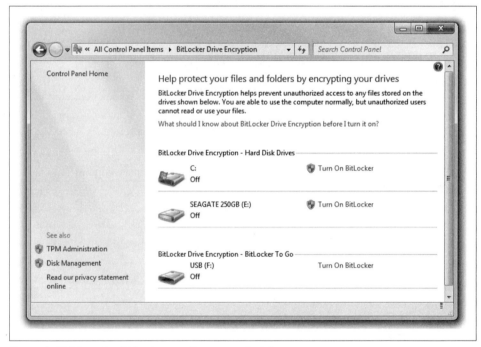

Figure 4-17. Managing BitLocker on all your attached drives

 Using BitLocker to encrypt your operating system drive also requires two partitions on the hard drive—one system partition (hidden boot partition) and one operating system partition. Fortunately, Windows 7 automatically creates these two partitions during the installation process.

For encrypting data drives, BitLocker requires the drive to be formatted using either the exFAT, FAT16, FAT32, or NTFS filesystems.

BitLocker To Go

BitLocker To Go is an extension of the BitLocker application that provides encryption support for removable hard disks and thumb drives.

 BitLocker To Go is available only in the Enterprise and Ultimate editions of Windows 7.

To turn on BitLocker To Go, simply insert your thumb drive into your computer, right-click the drive icon in Computer (see Figure 4-18) and select "Turn on BitLocker...".

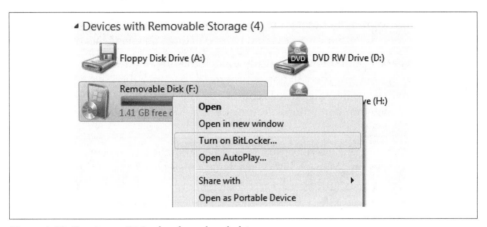

Figure 4-18. Turning on BitLocker for a thumb drive

Now you need to choose a way for the drive to be unlocked when it has been encrypted—using a password or a smartcard. The easiest way would be to choose a password; if you choose this option, supply a password. Click Next to proceed.

In the next step, you have a choice to store your recovery key to a file or print it out. The recovery key is used to temporarily unlock a BitLocker-encrypted drive in the event that you forgot the password. Choose the desired option and click Next.

You are now ready to encrypt your drive. Click the Start Encrypting button to begin the encryption.

Windows will now start to encrypt your drive. It will take some time, especially if you have a large-capacity thumb drive. When the encryption is done, a lock will appear on the drive icon (see Figure 4-19).

From now on, whenever you insert your thumb drive into your computer, you will be prompted to enter the password to unlock the drive. Enter the password and click the Unlock button to unlock the drive.

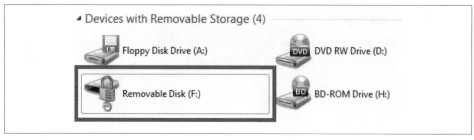

Figure 4-19. The BitLocker-encrypted thumb drive

If you insert a thumb drive encrypted with BitLocker To Go into a Windows XP computer, you will be prompted to enter the key to unlock the drive.

If you forgot your password, click the "I forgot my password" link. You will be prompted to enter the recovery key that you saved/printed earlier. Enter the recovery key and you will be granted temporary access to the drive before you change its password.

You also have the option to automatically unlock the drive on the current computer. If you choose this option, you will not be prompted to unlock the drive every time you insert the thumb drive into the current computer. You should choose this option only if you are sure that your computer is secure and that it is not easily accessible to other people.

You can change the BitLocker feature of a drive by right-clicking the drive icon in Computer and selecting Manage BitLocker. Figure 4-20 shows the options available.

Figure 4-20. Managing BitLocker on an encrypted drive

Encrypting File System (NTFS Encryption)

As you have seen, BitLocker and BitLocker To Go encrypt the entire drive to protect the integrity of your filesystems. However, sometimes you may need to encrypt just selected files (or folders), not the entire drive. To do this, you can make use of the Encrypting File System, also known as the NTFS Encryption feature of Windows 7.

 NTFS Encryption is available only in Windows 7 Professional, Enterprise, and Ultimate.

To encrypt a file (or folder), right-click its icon and select Properties. In the General tab, click the Advanced... button. Check the "Encrypt contents to secure data" checkbox (see Figure 4-21) and click OK twice.

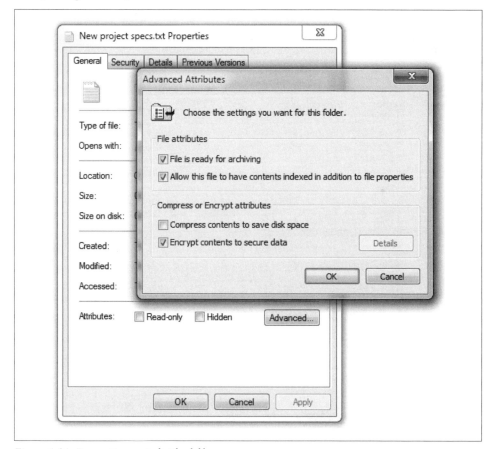

Figure 4-21. Encrypting an individual file

You will be asked if you want to encrypt the entire file itself, or encrypt its parent folder as well (recommended). Select the option you want and click OK.

The file will now be encrypted. If you click the Details button as shown previously in Figure 4-21, you will see that the file has been encrypted using a certificate bearing your name (this is created for you automatically).

When you select the certificate name, you will be able to back up the certificate to disk. Doing so allows you to pass your certificate to other users so that they can also access this encrypted file. However, giving your certificate to other users will allow them to access all your encrypted files and folders (that use the same certificate). So, think carefully before you give away your certificates.

See the section "Importing Certificates" on page 73 for more information on how to import certificates onto your computer.

To allow other users to access your encrypted file, click the Add... button to add the certificates provided by the users. A user who possesses the certificate contained in the certificates list (shown in Figure 4-22) will be able to access your encrypted file.

Figure 4-22. Viewing the user access list for the encrypted file

Creating Certificates

When you encrypt a file using NTFS Encryption, Windows 7 automatically creates an encryption certificate for you if you do not already have one. However, you can also manually create your own encryption certificate using the "Manage file encryption certificates" application (just type "Manage file encryption certificates" in the search box of the Start menu).

 By creating your own certificates, you can then encrypt different files using different certificates. Doing so allows you to share specific encrypted files with other users without compromising the integrity of other files.

When the application is launched, the window shown in Figure 4-23 should appear. Click Next to continue.

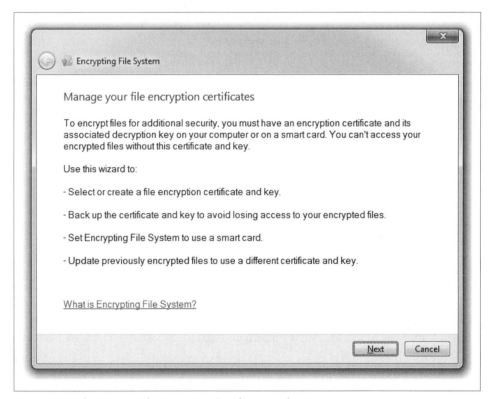

Figure 4-23. The Manage File Encryption Certificates application

If you already have a certificate created for you, you should see it now. To view other certificates on your computer, click the "Select certificate" button.

If you want to create a new certificate, choose the "Create a new certificate" option and click Next.

You will now choose the type of certificate you want to create (see Figure 4-24). If you do not have a smartcard, you should select the first option, where you will create a self-signed certificate stored on your computer. Click Next.

Figure 4-24. Selecting the type of certificate you want to create

Your certificate will now be created. On the next screen, you have the option to back up your certificate to storage. Supply a path and a password for the backup. Click Next to continue.

Now you have the option to update your encrypted files with the new certificate and key (all your encrypted files will now use this new certificate). Select the drives or folders containing the encrypted files and click Next.

That's it! Your certificate is now created. The certificate is saved as a file with the *.pfx* extension.

Importing Certificates

When you receive a *.pfx* certificate from someone else, you can import it into your own certificate store in Windows by double-clicking the *.pfx* file. When you double-click a *.pfx* file, the Certificate Import Wizard will appear. Click Next to proceed.

You will be asked to specify the location of the *.pfx* file. When done, click Next.

Enter the password that was used to protect the certificate and then click Next twice. Finally, if the importing is successful, click the Finish button.

Antispyware and Firewall Applications

As part of its Trustworthy Computing push, Microsoft is very serious about security in Windows. As such, all recent Windows operating systems come with several built-in tools to protect the users. Two tools that stand out are Windows Defender and Windows Firewall.

Windows Defender

Like Windows Vista, Windows 7 includes an antispyware program called Windows Defender. Windows Defender's role is to prevent, remove, and quarantine spyware in Windows.

 Windows Defender was previously known as Microsoft AntiSpyware. Windows Defender shipped with Windows Vista and is available as a free download for Windows XP and Windows Server 2003.

Windows Defender is located within the Control Panel (you can find it by typing "defender" in the Search box). Once Windows Defender is launched, you can start scanning your computer for spyware by clicking the Scan button (see Figure 4-25).

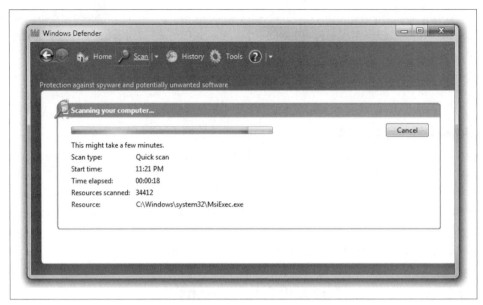

Figure 4-25. Scanning for spyware using Windows Defender

You can also configure Windows Defender to scan at regular intervals (see Figure 4-26) by selecting Tools→Options.

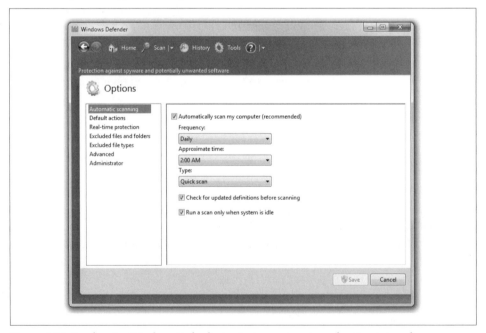

Figure 4-26. Configuring Windows Defender to start scanning at regular time intervals

Windows Firewall

First shipping in Windows XP and then Vista, the Windows Firewall is included in Windows 7 as well. Windows Firewall prevents unauthorized data from traveling between your computer and the network (such as the Internet).

 Windows Firewall was originally known as Internet Connection Firewall when it first shipped with Windows XP.

Like the Windows Defender, the Windows Firewall can be accessed via the Control Panel; select System and Security→Windows Firewall.

You can configure Windows Firewall to turn on or off depending on the network connections you are connected to—Home, Work, or Public. Home and Work are considered private networks; Public is considered a public network. Clicking the "Turn Windows Firewall on or off" link will bring you to the customization page shown in Figure 4-27.

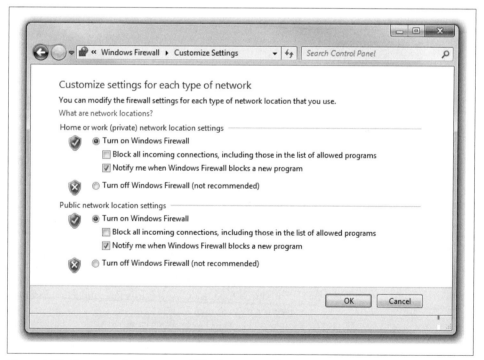

Figure 4-27. The customization page of Windows Firewall

If you have an application that is blocked by Windows Firewall, you can click the "Allow a program or feature through Windows Firewall" link to allow it to pass through the Windows Firewall explicitly (see Figure 4-28).

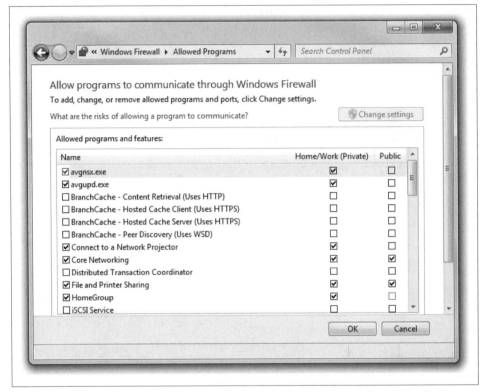

Figure 4-28. Granting permission so applications can pass through the Windows Firewall

Antivirus Tools

Despite Microsoft's commitment to security, there is one tool that is apparently missing in all Windows operating systems—antivirus tools.

Although there are many commercial antivirus tools available for the Windows platform, one of my personal favorites is AVG Anti-Virus (*http://free.avg.com*). AVG comes in three different versions: AVG Anti-Virus Free, AVG Anti-Virus Pro, and AVG Internet Security. The first version is free for private use.

Summary

In this chapter, you read about the various security features that ship with Windows 7. In particular, you have seen the use of:

- Action Center, the one-stop place where you will find all your system maintenance and security messages
- User Account Control, to manage the level of warnings you receive when changes are made to the system
- Credential Manager, to store credentials that you use to log in to websites and servers
- BitLocker drive encryption, to encrypt data on your hard drives as well as removable thumb drives
- Encrypting File System, to encrypt specific files on your filesystem
- Windows Defender and Windows Firewall, to block data traveling between your computer and the network

CHAPTER 5

Essential Applications

Another of the longstanding Windows traditions that Windows 7 abandoned is that it contains fewer bundled applications than its previous versions. For example, Microsoft Mail will not be available when you install Windows 7. Similarly, Messenger will also not be installed when you install Windows 7. Instead, Microsoft offers a suite of essential applications as a separate download. Doing so allows Microsoft to have separate release timelines for Windows and these essential applications. It also allows them to make these essential applications more easily available for earlier versions of Windows.

In the first part of this chapter, you will first see how you can install the suite of essential applications from Microsoft free of charge. We will then look at the suite of built-in applications that ship with Windows 7.

Windows Live Essentials

Windows Live is the brand name for a set of services and applications offered by Microsoft. Broadly speaking, Windows Live is made of two parts: Windows Live Services and Windows Live Essentials. Windows Live Services refers to hosted applications/services that you can use over the Web. A good example of a Windows Live Services application is Hotmail; another example would be MySpace. Windows Live Essentials, on the other hand, refers to a suite of applications that users can download and install on their Windows computers. Examples are Messenger, Mail, and Photo Gallery. This section will focus on Windows Live Essentials.

The Windows Live Essentials suite includes the following key applications (as well as some add-ins to other applications such as the Windows Live Toolbar for Internet Explorer):

- Messenger
- Mail
- Photo Gallery
- Writer

- Family Safety
- Movie Maker

To download Live Essentials, go to *http://download.live.com*. You can download the main installer application, which will allow you to choose and download your desired applications on demand (see Figure 5-1).

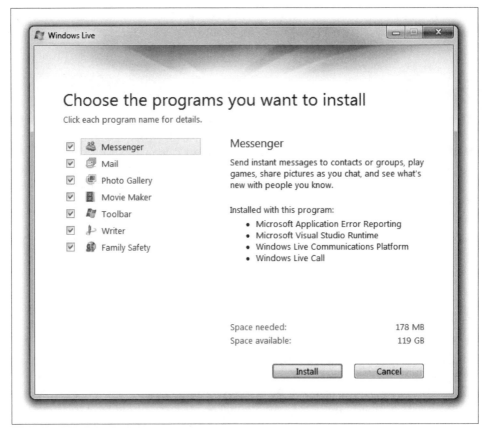

Figure 5-1. Download the desired applications in Live Essentials

Windows Live Messenger

Windows Live Messenger is an instant messaging application.

Windows Live Messenger offers the following functionalities:

- File transfers
- PC-to-PC and PC-to-phone calls

- Photo sharing
- Sending SMS messages

Using Live Messenger, you can also send messages to other users even when they are offline (see Figure 5-2).

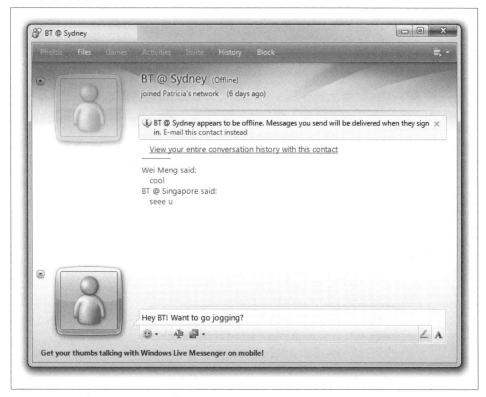

Figure 5-2. Sending messages to offline users

Windows Live Mail

Windows Live Mail is the successor to Outlook Express (shipped with Windows XP) and Windows Mail on Windows Vista. Using Live Mail, you can read and send email from one or more email accounts, including accounts from providers such as Hotmail, Gmail, Yahoo!, and more.

Live Mail supports the POP3, IMAP, and HTTP protocols. The last one is particularly important for Hotmail users, because that service requires the HTTP protocol in order to be able to read your email using a mail client (unless you subscribe to the Hotmail Premium service).

Also included with Mail are four other subapplications—Calendar, Contacts, Feeds, and Newsgroups (see Figure 5-3; you need to press the Alt key to reveal the menu).

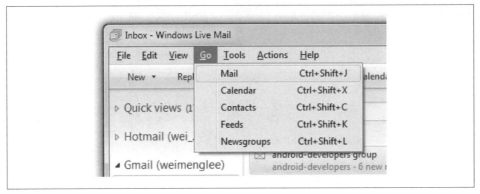

Figure 5-3. Four other subapplications included with Mail

When you click the Sign In button in the upper right, Windows Live Mail will:

- Allow you to use your Windows Live online contact list (via the Windows Live Contacts application) and see when senders are online in Messenger
- Sync with your Windows Live calendars

Windows Live Mail Versus Live Hotmail

The popular, free web-based email service Hotmail was once called Windows Live Mail. It has since been renamed Windows Live Hotmail. The name Windows Live Mail now refers to the desktop version of the email application.

Subscribing to Microsoft Communities

To subscribe to a newsgroup using Windows Live Mail, click the Newsgroup icon in the bottom left of the Windows Live Mail window (or make the menu visible with the Alt key, then select Go→Newsgroups). The first time you go to the Newsgroups section, you will see a message indicating that you are not subscribed to any newsgroup. Click the View Newsgroups button to see a list of available newsgroups from the Microsoft Communities (see Figure 5-4). Select the newsgroups that you are interested in and click Subscribe.

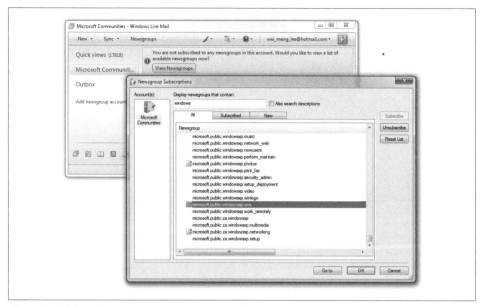

Figure 5-4. Subscribing to newsgroups in Microsoft Communities

You can now start reading the various postings from the newsgroup you have subscribed to (see Figure 5-5).

Figure 5-5. Reading the postings in the newsgroup

Working with the Calendar

To view your calendar in Windows Live Mail, click the Calendar icon in the bottom left of the Windows Live Mail window (or make the menu visible with the Alt key, then select Go→Calendar). The calendar will be displayed (see Figure 5-6).

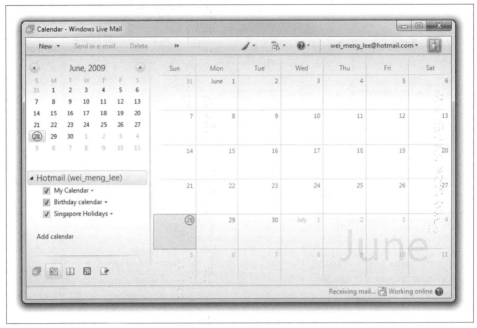

Figure 5-6. Viewing the calendar in Windows Live Mail

 By default, three calendars will be created for you: My Calendar (your personal calendar), Birthday calendar (your contacts' birthdays calendar), and <Location> Holidays (the holidays of the country you have selected).

You can create a new Calendar by clicking the "Add calendar" link, as shown in Figure 5-6. Creating a new calendar allows you to organize the entries according to specific occasions. For example, you might have a calendar for company meetings and another for family matters.

You can also share calendars that you have created with your friends or the public. Before you can share your calendar, you need to sign into Live.com. Click the Sign In button in the upper right of the Windows Live Mail Window (if you see your Windows Live ID listed there instead of a Sign In button, it means that you are already signed in).

However, to do so, you need to use the web-based version of Calendar. First, log in to *http://calendar.live.com*. You will be asked to sign in using your Live ID (the one that you signed into from within Windows Live Mail). Once you have signed in, you will be able to specify which calendar you want to share by clicking the Share link (see Figure 5-7). You can then specify whom you want to invite to subscribe to your calendar, and the selected recipients will receive an email invitation.

To immediately synchronize the calendars and events created in Windows Live Mail with the Calendar in Live.com, press F5.

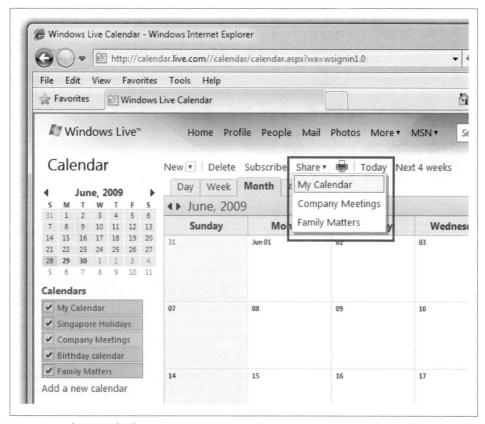

Figure 5-7. Sharing calendars in Live.com

Another interesting thing you can do with Windows Live Mail is subscribe to an online calendar. Subscribing to online calendars allows you to view the calendar of another party and be updated automatically when the party's calendar is updated.

To subscribe to a calendar published by other users/organizations, click the Subscribe link (see Figure 5-8).

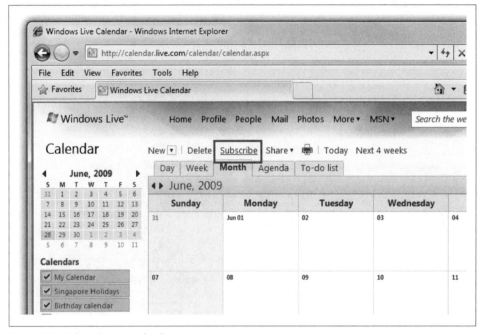

Figure 5-8. Subscribing to calendars

You will be asked to either subscribe from a public calendar via a URL or import an *.ics* file (see Figure 5-9).

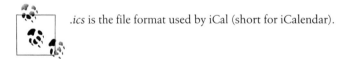 *.ics* is the file format used by iCal (short for iCalendar).

When you subscribe to a calendar via a URL, you will always get the updates performed by the calendar owner. An example of a calendar URL looks like this: *http:// cid-6d498f3bdb1fa52e.calendar.live.com/calendar/Trainings/index.html*. If you choose to import the calendar via an *.ics* file, then you will only get a static calendar (i.e., you won't see updates performed by the calendar owner).

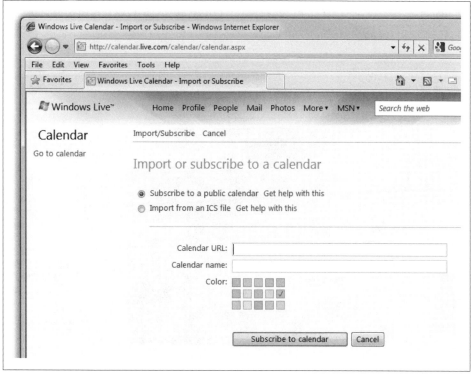

Figure 5-9. Ways to subscribe to a calendar

Calendars created in Live.com will be synchronized automatically with Windows Live Mail when you relaunch Windows Live Mail again (or simply press F5).

Windows Live Photo Gallery

Windows Live Photo Gallery is a photo management and photo sharing application that is tightly integrated with Windows Live Messenger. Using the Live Photo Gallery, you can organize your photos into folders, as well as tag photos and then upload them to Windows Live Photos and Flickr.

 Windows Live Photo Gallery is the successor to Vista's Windows Photo Gallery application.

Figure 5-10 shows how you can tag a photo with names of a friend (or yourself) and add descriptive tags to your photo.

Figure 5-10. Adding a tag to a photo

 The names of your friends are taken from Windows Live Messenger and Windows Live Contacts.

Windows Live Writer

Windows Live Writer is a blog-publishing application that allows you to publish your postings to blog publishing sites such as Blogger, WordPress, TypePad, and Windows Live Spaces.

When you first start Live Writer, you will be asked to create a new blog on Windows Live or use an existing blogging account. Once you have done this, you can use Writer to create a new posting and then publish it to your blogging account (see Figure 5-11).

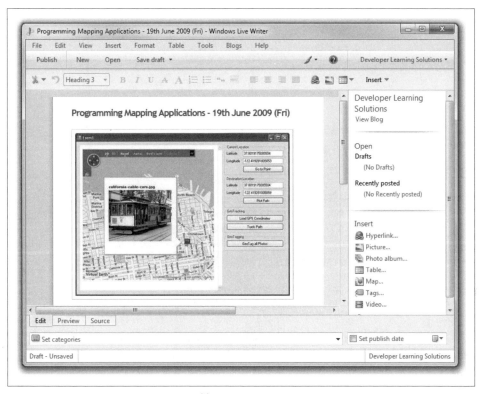

Figure 5-11. Using Live Writer to post a blog

A nice feature of Windows Live Writer is WYSIWYG editing, and also that it supports rich content like images, maps, videos, and all major text-editing features like tables, alignment, and spellchecking.

Windows Live Family Safety

Windows Live Family Safety is a parental control application that allows parents to monitor their children's activities on the Web. You can install Live Family Safety on all computers that your children use in your home.

To activate Windows Live Family Safety, you will first be asked to log in using your Windows Live ID (such as your Hotmail email account). Once you have logged in, you will see the screen shown in Figure 5-12.

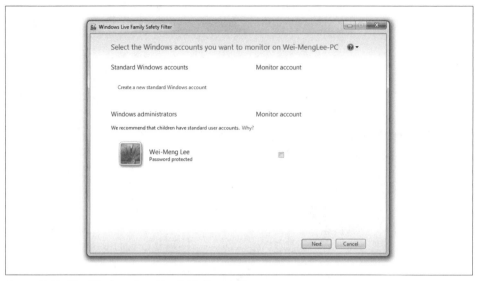

Figure 5-12. The Windows Live Family Safety application

Select the account(s) to monitor and click Next. You will be prompted to match the Windows account with the name in Family Safety. Once this is done, click Save. You will now see that the default filter is Basic, which means that only adult websites are blocked. To change the filter, go to *http://familysafety.live.com* and you will be able to change the filter type to Strict, Basic, or Custom (see Figure 5-13).

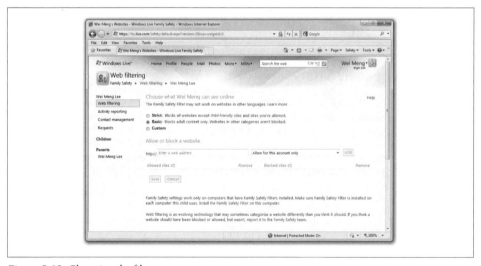

Figure 5-13. Changing the filter type

Once the filter is installed, if a child tries to visit a restricted website, he will see the screen shown in Figure 5-14.

Figure 5-14. Blocking a site that is restricted

In order for the child to visit the page, he will need a parent (the one who signed in to Live Family Safety) to authorize the page using the password supplied during the signing-in process. Alternatively, the child can also email the parent the request.

Windows Live Movie Maker

Windows Live Movie Maker is a video creating and editing application. It is the successor to the Windows Movie Maker included with Windows Vista.

 Windows Live Movie Maker requires a video card that is at least as powerful as the ATI Radeon 9500 or nVidia GeForce FX 5900.

The new Windows Live Movie Maker (see Figure 5-15) is now much more user-friendly. Using Live Movie Maker, you can save your movies in Windows Media as DVD quality or Windows Media portable device format.

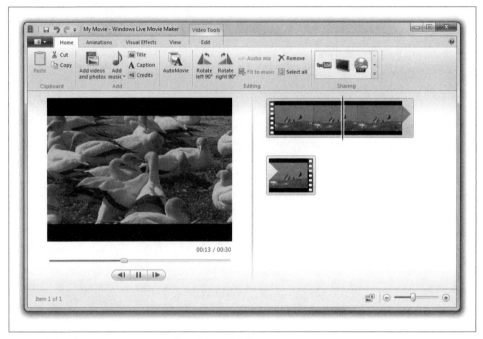

Figure 5-15. Creating movies using Live Movie Maker

Built-in Applications

In the previous section, you saw the suite of applications that you can download from Microsoft free of charge. Though the number of bundled applications has apparently decreased, there are still a number of cool applications shipped with Windows 7. The following sections describe some of them in detail.

Snipping Tool

Beginning with Windows Vista, Microsoft shipped an application called the Snipping Tool, which is included in Windows 7 as well. The Snipping Tool is a screen-capture tool.

Longtime users of Windows know that they can capture screenshots easily using the Print Scrn key (or Alt-Print Scrn for capturing the current active window) on the keyboard. But the Snipping Tool makes it easy for you to capture specific parts of your screen directly without needing to further edit your screenshots. It also allows you to directly save the screenshots to file.

To launch the Snipping Tool, select Start menu→Snipping Tool. You will see the window shown in Figure 5-16.

Figure 5-16. The Snipping Tool

Clicking the arrow next to the New button reveals four options in which you can capture your screenshots:

Free-form Snip
> You can capture your screen by simply moving your mouse to designate the area you want to capture; it can be of any shape.

Rectangular Snip
> You capture a rectangular portion of your screen.

Windows Snip
> You capture any of the opened windows on the screen.

Full-screen Snip
> You capture the entire screen. This works for multiple monitor setups, too.

Figure 5-17 shows the screenshot captured with the Snipping Tool. You can save the image to disk or email it. If you want to insert the captured image into another application (say, Word), click the Copy icon (third icon) and paste it into your target application.

Figure 5-17. The Snipping Tool with the screenshot captured

Sound Recorder

Windows 7 also includes another useful application called the Sound Recorder. As its name implies, it allows you to record sound and save it as an audio file. All you need is an audio device (such as a microphone plugged into the audio jack of your computer, or a webcam with a built-in microphone).

The user interface of the Sound Recorder is very simple (see Figure 5-18). It has a button labeled Start Recording, which starts the audio recording. The bar displayed next to it indicates the audio level (it moves as the audio input level changes).

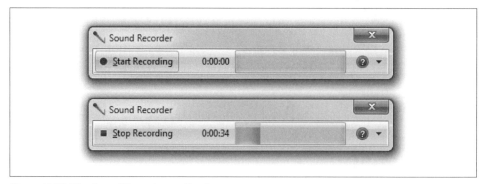

Figure 5-18. The Sound Recorder application

When you are done, click the Stop Recording button. You will be prompted to save the audio recorded as a *.wma* file.

Windows PowerShell

In Windows 7, the Windows PowerShell application is included by default. The Windows PowerShell is an extensible command-line shell application that executes applications written in its associated scripting languages, allowing IT administrators to easily automate and administer their IT infrastructure. Think of Windows PowerShell as the command prompt (with which most Windows users are familiar) on steroids—a very powerful one indeed.

 Windows PowerShell is available as a separate download for Windows XP and Vista users.

To launch Windows PowerShell, type "Windows PowerShell" in the Start menu text box.

Using the Windows PowerShell, you can issue commands that you normally use with your command prompt window, such as dir:

```
Windows PowerShell
Copyright (C) 2009 Microsoft Corporation. All rights reserved.

PS C:\Users\Wei-Meng Lee> dir


    Directory: C:\Users\Wei-Meng Lee


Mode                LastWriteTime     Length Name
----                -------------     ------ ----
d-r--          5/2/2009    2:49 PM           Contacts
d-r--          6/22/2009   6:48 AM           Desktop
d-r--          6/20/2009   2:28 PM           Documents
d-r--          6/19/2009  12:02 PM           Downloads
d-r--          5/20/2009   9:06 AM           Favorites
d-r--          5/2/2009    2:49 PM           Links
d-r--          5/2/2009    2:49 PM           Music
d-r--          6/14/2009  10:07 PM           Pictures
d-r--          5/2/2009    3:42 PM           Saved Games
d-r--          6/9/2009    2:33 PM           Searches
d----          6/28/2009   9:49 AM           Tracing
d-r--          5/2/2009    2:49 PM           Videos
d-r--          6/20/2009   1:51 PM           Virtual Machines


PS C:\Users\Wei-Meng Lee>
```

When you issue the `dir` command, PowerShell actually translates it into the name of a cmdlet (Windows 7 has more than 100 cmdlets), which is a programming script. The `dir` command is an alias of the `Get-ChildItem` cmdlet.

The following example shows how you can take the directory listing of the Windows directory and then pipe it into another cmdlet named *format-list*, which displays in detail the information of each directory and file:

```
PS C:\Windows> dir | format-list


    Directory: C:\Windows



Name          : addins
CreationTime  : 4/22/2009 4:55:52 PM
LastWriteTime : 4/22/2009 4:55:52 PM
LastAccessTime : 4/22/2009 4:55:52 PM

Name          : AppCompat
CreationTime  : 4/22/2009 2:17:25 PM
LastWriteTime : 5/16/2009 6:47:19 AM
LastAccessTime : 5/16/2009 6:47:19 AM

Name          : AppPatch
CreationTime  : 4/22/2009 2:17:25 PM
LastWriteTime : 4/22/2009 5:01:13 PM
LastAccessTime : 4/22/2009 5:01:13 PM

Name          : assembly
CreationTime  : 4/22/2009 2:17:25 PM
LastWriteTime : 5/28/2009 3:25:15 AM
LastAccessTime : 5/28/2009 3:25:15 AM

Name          : Boot
CreationTime  : 4/22/2009 2:17:26 PM
LastWriteTime : 4/22/2009 4:55:52 PM
LastAccessTime : 4/22/2009 4:55:52 PM

Name          : Branding
CreationTime  : 4/22/2009 2:17:26 PM
LastWriteTime : 4/22/2009 4:55:52 PM
LastAccessTime : 4/22/2009 4:55:52 PM

...
...

Name          : write.exe
Length        : 9216
CreationTime  : 4/22/2009 11:39:18 AM
LastWriteTime : 4/22/2009 1:19:45 PM
LastAccessTime : 4/22/2009 11:39:18 AM
VersionInfo   : File:             C:\Windows\write.exe
                InternalName:     write
```

```
                    OriginalFilename: write
                    FileVersion:       6.1.7100.0 (winmain_win7rc.090421-1700)
                    FileDescription:  Windows Write
                    Product:          Microsoftr Windowsr Operating System
                    ProductVersion:   6.1.7100.0
                    Debug:            False
                    Patched:          False
                    PreRelease:       False
                    PrivateBuild:     False
                    SpecialBuild:     False
                    Language:         English (United States)


Name            : _default.pif
Length          : 707
CreationTime    : 4/22/2009 9:29:14 AM
LastWriteTime   : 3/20/2009 11:42:51 PM
LastAccessTime  : 4/22/2009 9:29:14 AM
VersionInfo     : File:              C:\Windows\_default.pif
                    InternalName:
                    OriginalFilename:
                    FileVersion:
                    FileDescription:
                    Product:
                    ProductVersion:
                    Debug:            False
                    Patched:          False
                    PreRelease:       False
                    PrivateBuild:     False
                    SpecialBuild:     False
                    Language:
```

 For more information on Windows PowerShell, refer to *Windows PowerShell Cookbook* by Lee Holmes (O'Reilly).

Windows Photo Viewer

Windows 7 ships with the Photo Viewer application for viewing images. Using the Photo Viewer, you can perform the following actions:

- Display the next/previous photo in the same folder
- Change the magnification of the photo
- Print the photo to a printer
- Send the photo to a printing service (Print→Order prints...)
- Email the photo to a friend

- Burn the photo to a data disc
- Open the photo using other applications such as Paint, Windows Media Center, and so on

 Windows Photo Viewer is automatically launched when you double-click on an image.

The best part of Photo Viewer is its ability to make video DVDs using the bundled Windows DVD Maker. To create a video DVD using your photos, select Burn→Video DVD. This will launch the Windows DVD Maker. Click the "Add items" button to select all the photos and videos that you want to add to your video DVD. Click Next to continue.

You can select the style of the menu to apply to your DVD, as well change the title (see Figure 5-19). You can also add background music to accompany your photos. When you are ready, click the Burn button to burn the photos onto a DVD.

Figure 5-19. Customizing the content of your DVD

Windows DVD Maker will now proceed to burn the photos onto the DVD. Figure 5-20 shows the DVD playing in Windows Media Player.

Figure 5-20. Playing the video DVD using Windows Media Player

 You can also play your DVD using a conventional DVD player.

Windows Disc Image Burner

Windows 7 has a built-in disc burning tool that makes writing ISO or IMG images to CD and DVDs very easy.

To burn an ISO or IMG image to disc, right-click the image name and select "Burn disc image" (see Figure 5-21).

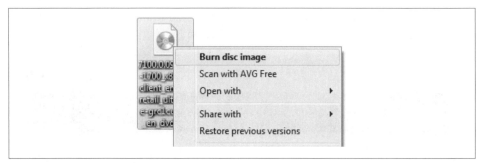

Figure 5-21. Disc burning is now built right into Windows

The Windows Disc Image Burner will now appear (see Figure 5-22). Select the drive to burn the image and check the "Verify disc after burning" checkbox to ensure that the disc is written correctly. Then click the Burn button to burn the disc.

Figure 5-22. Selecting the drive to burn the image

One cool thing about the Windows Disc Image Burner is that when it detects a DVD-RW with content on it, it will prompt you to confirm whether you want to erase its content and write new content onto it. This is very helpful, as it prevents users from accidentally erasing important data on the disc.

Mounting ISO Images

Although it is neat to be able to burn an ISO image to CD or DVD natively in Windows 7, it would be even better to be able to mount ISO images as virtual drives, which would allow users to access the content of the image just as if they were accessing the content of an inserted CD or DVD. Unfortunately, Windows 7 does not ship with the tool for mounting ISO images. For this purpose, my personal favorite is the free Virtual CloneDrive from SlySoft (*http://www.slysoft.com/en/virtual-clonedrive.html*). Once Virtual CloneDrive is installed, you can launch it by right-clicking an ISO image and selecting Open with→Mount Files with Virtual CloneDrive (see Figure 5-23).

Once the image is mounted, you will see an additional drive in Computer.

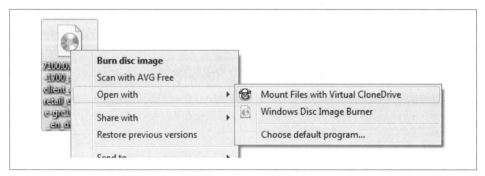

Figure 5-23. Mounting an ISO image with Virtual CloneDrive

Windows Media Center

Windows 7 Home Premium (and higher) editions now ship with Windows Media Center. Using Windows Media Center, you can watch and record TV programs, play DVDs, listen to music, share your digital photos, and more.

If you wish to watch TV programs on your computer, you also need a TV tuner card. A remote control that works with Windows Media Center will greatly enhance your experience.

One nice improvement in Windows Media Center in Windows 7 is that you can now continue to watch your video while you navigate to other sections of the application (see Figure 5-24).

You can also use Windows Media Center to view your photos (see Figure 5-25).

Figure 5-24. You can continue watching a program while you select from other menus

Figure 5-25. Viewing photos using Windows Media Center

Math Input Panel

One very geeky application included with Windows 7 is the Math Input Panel (Start→All Programs→Accessories→Math Input Panel). The Math Input Panel allows you to literally "write" mathematical equations on the screen so that they can be transformed into a format recognizable by applications (such as Word, OpenOffice, and StarOffice) that support the MathML format.

Figure 5-26 shows that as you write the mathematical equation, it is instantly parsed by the Math Input Panel and transformed into a recognizable format. Click the Insert button to insert the equation into your word processor.

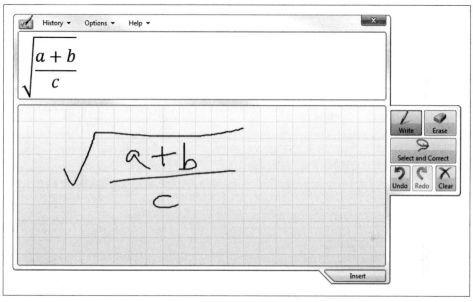

Figure 5-26. Using the Math Input Panel to create math equations

The equation from Figure 5-26 is then generated by the Math Input Panel (see Figure 5-27).

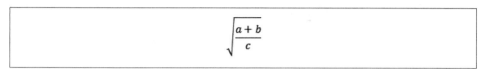

Figure 5-27. The equation generated by the Math Input Panel

The Math Input Panel is best used with a touchscreen or a tablet, where you can use a pen to write your mathematical equations quickly.

XPS Viewer

In Windows Vista, you had to download the XPS Essentials Pack in order to obtain the XPS Viewer. In Windows 7, the XPS Viewer is bundled together with the OS.

What Is XPS?

The XML Paper Specification (XPS) is a page-description language and fixed-document format specification developed by Microsoft. XPS allows you to preserve your document's fidelity while ensuring portability. XPS is similar in function to PDF, except that PDF is a database of objects and XPS is based on XML.

The XPS Viewer (see Figure 5-28) in Windows 7 allows you to sign your documents with your own digital certificates.

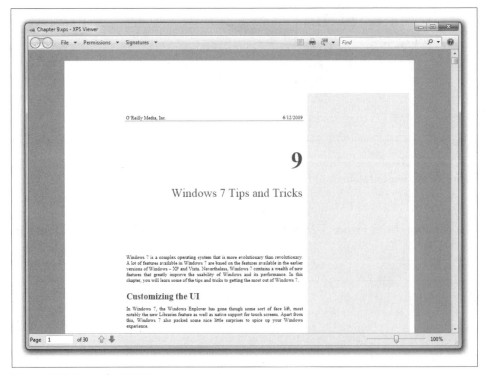

Figure 5-28. Using the XPS Viewer

Like Windows Vista, Windows 7 also includes the XPS Document Writer by default. Using the XPS Document Writer, you can create XPS documents easily by simply printing to the XPS Document Writer. When you print to the XPS Document Writer, you will be asked to provide a name to save the XPS file.

Sticky Notes

In Windows Vista, Windows Sidebar comes with a built-in gadget called Sticky Notes. In Windows 7, the Sticky Notes gadget is no longer available. In place of it is the Sticky Notes application (see Figure 5-29; available through the Start menu).

Figure 5-29. Using Sticky Notes in Windows 7

The Sticky Notes application has some useful functions, such as:

- Adding new sticky notes or deleting existing ones
- Changing the color of the note
- Resizing the notes

Calculator

The old Calculator application available in all versions of Windows finally gets a huge makeover in this release of Windows. Calculator now supports four modes:

- Standard
- Scientific
- Programmer (new)
- Statistics (new)

Besides the two additional new modes, Calculator also features worksheets, in which you can perform the following calculations:

- Unit conversion
- Date calculation

- Mortgages
- Vehicle leases
- Fuel economy (mpg)
- Fuel economy (L/100km)

The Programmer mode allows users to quickly enter values using different bases (such as binary, octal, decimal, or hexadecimal) and view its equivalent in binary (see Figure 5-30). You can also perform operations on numbers, such as AND, OR, and XOR.

Figure 5-30. The Calculator in Programmer mode

The new worksheets feature in Calculator is a big plus for a lot of Windows users. Instead of fumbling to work out some common calculations (like fuel efficiency, mortgage repayment, and so on), you can now easily calculate them using the Calculator (see Figure 5-31).

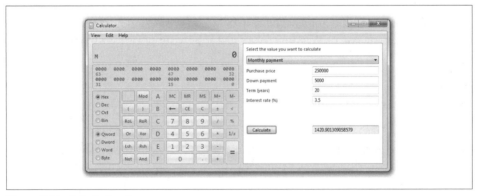

Figure 5-31. Calculating the mortgage repayment

Microsoft WordPad

When Office 2007 was released, the new ribbon interface created quite a stir in the world of Office users. Now, in Windows 7, you have the same ribbon interface in WordPad (see Figure 5-32).

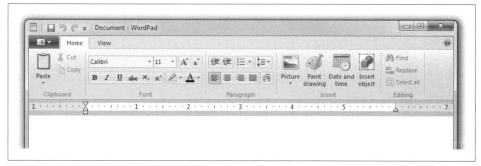

Figure 5-32. The ribbon interface in WordPad

Besides the change in user interface, WordPad also includes support for OpenXML and OpenDocument Text (used by the free OpenOffice.org Writer program) files.

Microsoft Paint

Paint is the next application bundled with Windows 7 to receive a ribbon interface UI makeover (see Figure 5-33). With the new ribbon interface, Paint is now much easier to use.

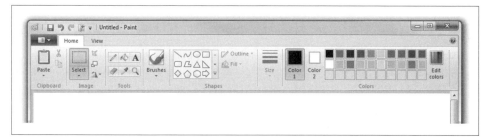

Figure 5-33. The ribbon interface in Paint

Windows Media Player 12

Windows 7 also ships with a new Media Player: Windows Media Player 12.

Windows Media Player 12 is largely similar to its previous versions, but one of its key features is its ability to stream music from another computer using the new HomeGroup feature of Windows 7. For more information on streaming music using HomeGroup and Windows Media Player, refer to Chapter 3.

Summary

In this chapter, you have seen the numerous applications that you can download and install from the Windows Live Essentials suite of applications. This suite of applications offers much useful functionality that you would otherwise have to buy. Though Windows 7 has drastically reduced the number of bundled applications, there are still gems that ship with Windows 7.

CHAPTER 6

Internet Explorer 8

Windows 7 ships with the new Internet Explorer 8 (IE8). IE8 builds on the foundation of IE7 and this latest release contains many useful enhancements in the areas of usability, privacy, and security.

In this chapter, you will learn about some of the innovations in IE8 and how they affect the way you surf the Web.

Usability

The first major noticeable improvement in IE8 is usability. Microsoft has taken pains to improve the usability of IE8 by adding the following features:

- Smarter Address bar that lists all the relevant sites you have visited by searching through your History, Favorites, and RSS Feeds
- Enhanced functionality of tabbed browsing by color-coding related tabs
- Support for older websites by displaying them using IE7 through the Compatibility View
- A much more usable Find feature to make searching for phrases on the web page easy
- Ability to visually search for items from providers like Wikipedia.com and Amazon.com
- Web Slices to help users monitor constantly changing web content
- Accelerators, which integrate commonly used functions into the browser so that users can perform common actions with a single mouse-click

Smart Address Bar

The Address bar in IE8 is now much smarter than its predecessor. In addition to typing websites' URLs, you can now type in keywords and it will search across your History, Favorites, and RSS Feeds and display all matching sites that you have visited previously (see Figure 6-1).

Figure 6-1. The smarter Address bar

This feature is very useful for finding pages that you have visited previously but whose URLs you cannot remember.

Enhanced Tabbed Browsing and Grouping

Prior to IE7, IE users were clamoring for tabbed browsing, which was a feature already available in competing browsers like Firefox and Opera. However, with tabbed browsing in IE7, things soon got out of control. You suddenly had tons of tabs on your browser window, and it was quite a task to manage them.

In IE8, when you create a new tab from an existing tab (for example, by right-clicking a link and selecting Open in New Tab), the new tab (and the existing tab) will be color-coded to help you visually group them together. Figure 6-2 shows two tab groups, each with two tab pages.

Figure 6-2. Tabs are color-coded to help you visually group them

The color-coding on the tabs will go away if you rearrange the tabs.

When you right-click one of the tabs, you can close the current selected tab, close the entire tab group, or ungroup the current tab from the current group (see Figure 6-3).

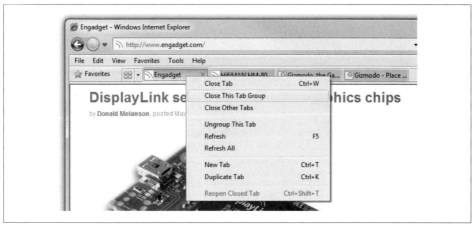

Figure 6-3. You can perform various actions with the tab groups

When you start a new tab, IE8 will provide several options with which you can open previously closed tabs as well as reopen the last browsing session (see Figure 6-4).

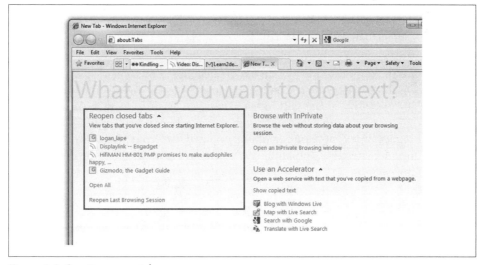

Figure 6-4. Creating a new tab page

The "Reopen closed tabs" option allows you to reopen all the tab pages that you have closed during the current browsing session. The Reopen Last Browsing Session option opens all the page(s) that you opened during your previous browsing session (before you closed your IE window).

Compatibility View

IE8 supports Compatibility View, which allows sites not optimized for IE8 to be displayed the way IE7 would have displayed them. This corrects problems such as misaligned text, images, and text boxes. To force a site to be displayed in IE7 mode, click the Compatibility View button located next to the URL of the site (see Figure 6-5).

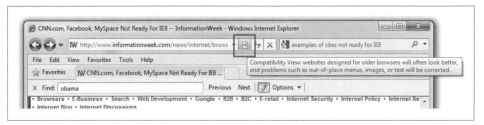

Figure 6-5. Forcing a site to display in IE7 mode using Compatibility View

What does it mean for a site to be unoptimized for IE8? Technically, IE8 is more up-to-date with modern web standards than IE7. However, some older sites that were optimized for IE7 relied on idiosyncrasies in how IE7 interpreted modern web standards. So, although IE8 should be more standards-compliant, there are still some websites that relied on IE-specific workarounds that don't look quite as good under IE8 as they did under IE7.

You also have the option to maintain a list of sites that need to be displayed in compatibility view. To do so, go to the Command bar and select Tools→Compatibility View Settings. You can now add the URL of sites that you want to view in Compatibility View (see Figure 6-6). Observe that in this window, you have several options for viewing pages in Compatibility View. You can obtain updated lists from Microsoft, disable IE8 to display Intranet sites in Compatibility View, or force all pages to be displayed in Compatibility View.

When viewing intranet pages, IE8 will automatically render the content using IE7 Standards mode. This is done to ensure maximum compatibility, as many intranet apps are still based on IE7. Hence the Compatibility View button will not be shown for Intranet pages.

Figure 6-6. Maintaining a list of sites to display in Compatibility View

Find on Page

One of the most frustrating features in IE7 (as well as previous versions) was the Find feature. Anyone who has used this feature knows that you needed to scroll the page to the top before you could start searching for the things you want. For a long time, IE has been playing catchup with browsers like Safari and Firefox, and finally in IE8, the Find feature that most users are waiting for is finally here.

To find a word or phrase on the page, press Ctrl-F (or go to Edit→Find on this Page...) and type the word or phrase you want to search for. Once the word or phrase is found, you will see the result bar shown in Figure 6-7.

All occurrences of the word or phrase are highlighted in yellow and the current word is highlighted in blue. To move to the next or previous occurrence of the phrase, click the Previous or the Next button.

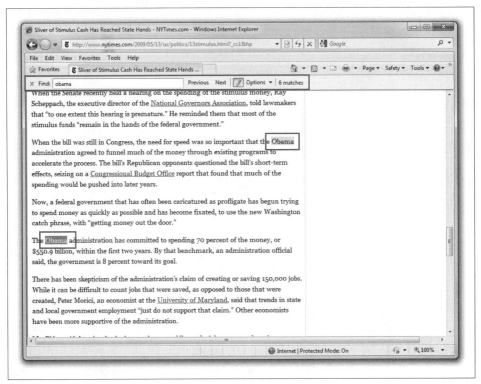

Figure 6-7. The new Find feature in IE

Improved Search

Searching in IE8 has now been improved. Microsoft is partnering with various search providers to provide "visual searches." For example, you can visually search Amazon.com's huge library of books from within IE. All you need to do is to add the Amazon Search Suggestion search provider by clicking the option arrow to the right of the search field, selecting Find More Providers, and adding the search provider (see Figure 6-8).

As you type, the search provider (Amazon.com in Figure 6-9) will return the search results visually. You can also switch between the different search providers you have installed by clicking the icons below the search result.

Visual Search Providers

Currently, the following search providers support visual search:

- The *New York Times* Instant Search
- Wikipedia Visual Search
- Amazon Search Suggestions
- eBay Visual Search
- Bing Search Suggestions
- Freebase Visual Search
- Bidtopia Search Suggestions

Figure 6-8. Adding new search providers to IE

Figure 6-9. Visual search in Amazon.com

 One neat trick with IE is that the web address field is also a search box—just type the search string in it and the default search provider configured in IE will perform a search.

Web Slices

IE8 supports a new feature called *Web Slices*. Basically, Web Slices allows you to automatically monitor changes in the content of some pages without needing to revisit the page. Consider the case of bidding for an item on eBay. If you are currently bidding for an item, you would be very interested in monitoring its bids closely so that you know the latest price. Rather than refreshing the page continuously, IE8 can do that for you and alert you when the content of the page changes.

Not All Sites Support Web Slices

Not all the websites out there on the Internet support Web Slices. When IE loads a page, it scans for the following elements in order to determine whether Web Slices is supported:

- The attribute `class=hslice` and the `id` attribute, like this:

    ```
    <divclass="hslice"id="result">
    ```

- At least one child element with the `entry-title` class name, like this:

    ```
    <div class="hslice" id="result">
            <h2 class="entry-title">Bidding for ...</h2>
            ...
        </div>
    ```

When you go to sites that support Web Slices, you will see the Web Slices icon appear as your mouse moves over sections of the page. The RSS button will also turn into the Web Slices icon. See the two highlighted icons in Figure 6-10.

Figure 6-10. Viewing pages that support Web Slices

When you click the Web Slices icon, you will be asked whether you want to view it from the Favorites bar (see Figure 6-11). Click the Add to Favorites Bar button to add the Web Slices.

Figure 6-11. Adding a Web Slice

You can now view the Web Slice in the Favorites bar. Clicking it will display the portion of the page (see Figure 6-12). When the content of the Web Slice has changed, the item in the Favorites bar will be displayed in bold and its background color will change.

Figure 6-12. Accessing the Web Slice on the Favorites bar

One popular site that supports Web Slices is eBay (see Figure 6-13).

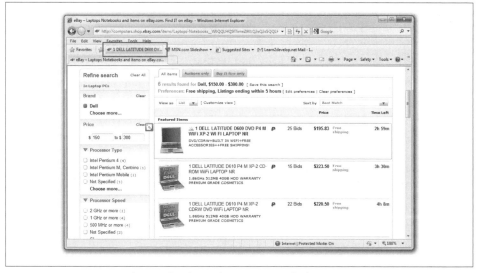

Figure 6-13. eBay is a good example of sites that support Web Slices

To customize the behavior of Web Slices, go to the Command bar and select Tools→Internet Options. Under the Content tab, click the Settings button in the Feeds and Web Slices section (see Figure 6-14). You can now configure the frequency of the updates (ranging from once every 15 minutes to once every week).

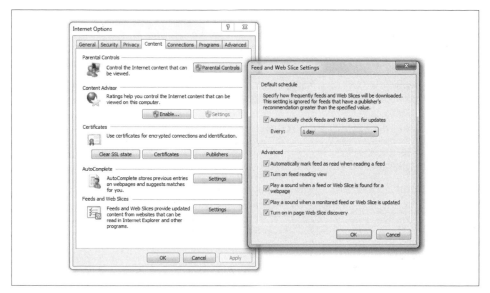

Figure 6-14. Customizing Web Slices

Accelerators

Imagine that you are searching for the address of a particular location. Once the address is found, you would most likely copy the address and navigate to Google Maps (or LiveSearch Maps) to check out the map of the location. Wouldn't it be easier if IE simply provided a link to automatically do just that?

Enter *accelerators*, a feature in IE8. Accelerators help you quickly accomplish tasks without needing to navigate to other websites. For example, if you want to check the map of a location, highlight the address (see Figure 6-15), click the blue accelerator icon displayed on the screen, and select "Map with Bing" accelerator.

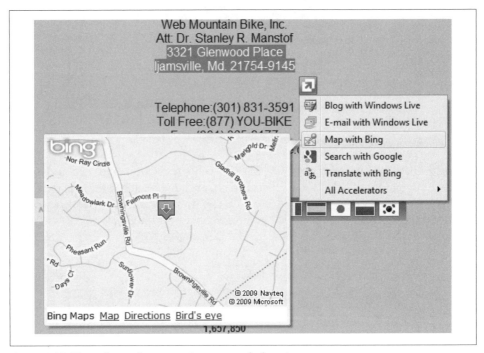

Figure 6-15. Using the accelerator to view a map of a location

The map of the selected address will now be displayed.

Another useful accelerator is the translation service provided by Live Search. Figure 6-16 shows the translation of a Japanese phrase to English.

Figure 6-16. Using accelerator to translate from Japanese to English

You can add more accelerators to IE8 by right-clicking any web page, choosing All Accelerators, and clicking Find More Accelerators.

Privacy

Privacy has always been a big concern for web browser makers as well as users. In IE8, Microsoft has taken one step forward in beefing up privacy through these features:

InPrivate Browsing
> Allows you to view websites without leaving behind any trace on your computer. The sites you visited and data you submitted will not be saved after you are done with the session. This is ideal for surfing on shared or public computers.

InPrivate Filtering
> Allows you to block code that websites often use to track your surfing pattern.

Although Microsoft has introduced these two features to enhance the privacy of its users, it has also introduced another new feature that makes some users uneasy. The Suggested Sites feature uses the information from sites you have visited to introduce some other sites to you that you may be interested in. Although this is a cool feature, some users are uncomfortable with Microsoft knowing too much about their surfing patterns.

InPrivate Browsing

InPrivate Browsing is very useful in a public environment in which you do not want others to know the pages you have visited. Some good examples are checking your email or performing banking transactions using a public computer, such as at the airport. With InPrivate Browsing, IE8 does not store information about the sites that you visit after the InPrivate Browsing session is closed. Such information includes cookies, temporary Internet files, web page history, form data, and passwords.

To activate InPrivate Browsing, click the Safety button in the Command bar and select InPrivate Browsing (see Figure 6-17).

Figure 6-17. Enabling InPrivate Browsing

 You can also activate InPrivate Browsing by clicking the "Open an In-Private Browsing window" link when you create a new empty tab in IE8.

A new window will be created (see Figure 6-18). Notice the label "InPrivate" displayed next to the address bar.

All tabs created in an InPrivate Browsing window are protected by InPrivate Browsing. InPrivate Browsing is turned off when you close the window.

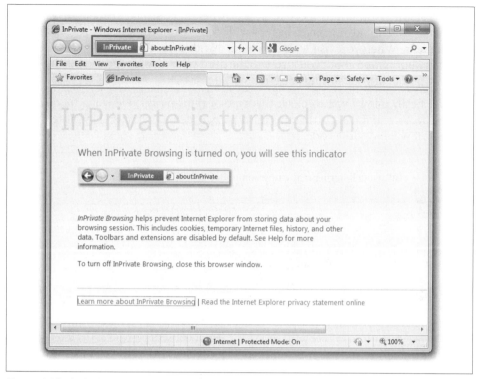

Figure 6-18. An InPrivate Browsing window

InPrivate Filtering

Over the years, websites have developed many different techniques to track their visitors' profiles. In the early years, websites tracked the IP addresses of users who visited their sites. By collecting the IP addresses of their users, websites were able to learn more about the surfing and usage patterns of their users. However, IP addresses tend to change, and hence, capturing users' IP addresses was not a very effective way of tracking them.

To overcome this, websites turned to cookies. When you visit a site, the site will save a small chunk of data on your computer, known as a cookie. When you revisit the site, the cookie will be sent back to the website, thereby allowing the website to know that you are a returning visitor. Though using cookies is a good way to track visitors, it is not cross-domain usable. The web browser will send back only a cookie created by the originating website. For example, if you visit *ebay.com* and then visit *ebay.com.sg*, there is no way for *ebay.com.sg* to know that you have visited *ebay.com*, as the cookie created by *ebay.com* won't be sent back to *ebay.com.sg*.

To overcome the restrictions of cookies, sites owners have turned to third-party content providers, generally advertisers, which provide code that websites can embed into their own content. When you visit a site embedded with code from a third-party content provider, information about you is sent to the third-party content provider, which then creates a profile of your surfing pattern.

IE8 specifically allows you to block this type of third-party code using the InPrivate Filtering feature. If it detects that this third-party code has been used by more than 10 websites, it will block the code.

 InPrivate Filtering may cause some sites to load incorrectly.

To turn on InPrivate Filtering, select the Safety button from the Command bar and select InPrivate Filtering (see Figure 6-19).

When you turn on InPrivate Filtering, by default, all detected content providers that are used by more than 10 sites are automatically blocked. If you want to manually configure which content providers to block, select the InPrivate Filtering Settings item from the Safety button. Figure 6-20 shows the list of content providers detected by IE8. You can manually select which content providers to block, as well as change the number of websites threshold.

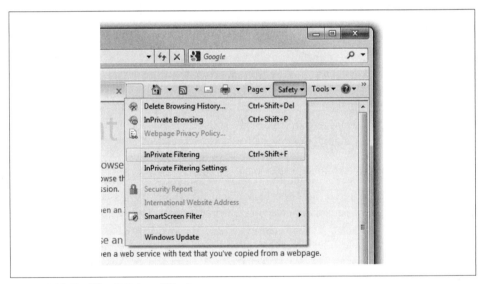

Figure 6-19. Enabling InPrivate Filtering

Figure 6-20. Changing the settings of the InPrivate Filtering feature

Suggested Sites

IE8 has a new service called Suggested Sites. Based on the current web page you are viewing, IE recommends other sites that are similar.

To turn on Suggested Sites, click the Suggested Sites button in the Favorites bar (select Tools→Toolbars→Favorites Bar if it is not visible) and click the "Turn on Suggested Sites" button (see Figure 6-21).

Figure 6-21. Turning on Suggested Sites

You will be asked to confirm this action. Click Yes (see Figure 6-22).

Figure 6-22. Confirming that you want to turn on Suggested Sites

Once Suggested Sites is turned on, you can now navigate to a site and click the Suggested Sites button to view other sites that are similar to the current one you are viewing (see Figure 6-23).

Figure 6-23. Displaying other websites that are similar to the one that you are viewing now

Note that Suggested Sites does not work for all sites.

Suggested Sites and Privacy Concerns

Though Suggested Sites sounds like a very useful feature in IE8, you need to be aware of how it works if you are concerned about your surfing privacy. In order for Suggested Sites to work, the URL of the sites that you have visited will be sent to Microsoft together with data such as your IP address, browser type, and regional and language settings. Microsoft has assured users that it will never use that data for targeted advertising, but privacy advocates are concerned that the data collected might be exploited by hackers. Website operators also run the risk of their users being lured away to rival sites.

 To turn off Suggested Sites, go to the Tools menu in the Command bar and deselect Suggested Sites.

Security

On the security front, Microsoft has made some UI tweaks to IE to encourage users to be more conscious of the sites they are visiting while at the same time adding new filters to help detect malicious websites.

Domain Highlighting

In IE8, the domain name in the URL is highlighted to draw your attention to the site you are visiting. As shown in Figure 6-24, it is apparent that the URL of the site is *oreillynet.com*, as it is highlighted in black while the rest of the URL is in gray.

Figure 6-24. Highlighting the domain name in the address bar

SmartScreen Filter

In IE7, Microsoft introduced the Phishing Filter, via which IE will try to warn users when they attempt to visit known phishing sites. In IE8, Microsoft has replaced the Phishing Filter with a feature called the SmartScreen Filter, which is still essentially a phishing filter, but with some advancement:

- Improved user interface
- Better performance
- Antimalware support

When a phishing site is detected, IE8 will display the warning page shown in Figure Figure 6-25.

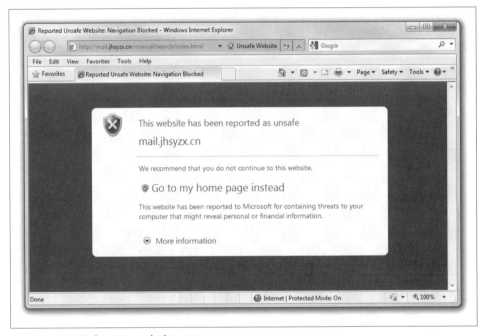

Figure 6-25. IE8 detecting a phishing site

You can also manually check whether a site contains threats by clicking the Safety button and then selecting SmartScreen Filter→Check This Website (see Figure 6-26). IE8 will check the URL against the list of suspected sites from its database.

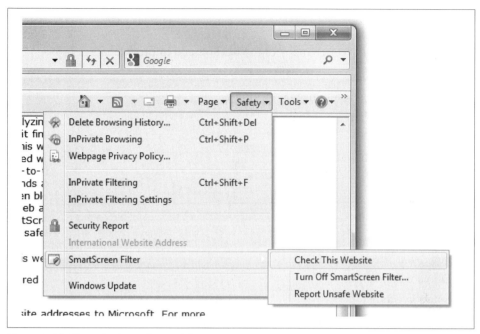

Figure 6-26. Using the SmartScreen Filter

You will also find options on the menu to turn off the SmartScreen filter or report unsafe websites.

Cross Site Scripting (XSS) Filter

IE8 also incorporates the XSS filter, which has the ability to prevent cross-site scripting, a security vulnerability found in web applications that allows code to be injected by malicious web users into pages viewed by others.

The XSS Filter can be turned on or off via Tools→Internet Options→Security→Custom Level→Enable XSS Filter.

To experience the XSS Filter in action, navigate to *http://www.ie8demos.com/tryit/* and click the Cross Site Scripting Filter link. When cross-site scripting is detected, IE8 will automatically block the malicious script from executing.

Summary

In this chapter, you have seen many of the features and improvements in IE8:

- Smart Address bar
- Enhanced tabbed browsing and grouping
- Compatibility View
- Find on Page
- Improved search
- Web Slices
- Accelerators
- InPrivate Browsing
- InPrivate Filtering
- Suggested Sites
- Domain highlighting
- SmartScreen Filter

With each revision, Microsoft is making sure that it stays ahead in the browser war. For end users, this can be only good news.

CHAPTER 7

Using Windows XP Mode

When Microsoft introduced Windows Vista, many users were very upset to discover that some of their older applications did not work correctly in Vista (some application vendors did not upgrade their applications for Vista, or charged more for new versions than users were willing to pay). As such, a lot of users (and businesses) cited this as a reason for not upgrading to Vista.

Microsoft realized the severity of this problem and hopes to solve it in Windows 7 by providing a feature known as *Windows XP Mode* (XPM). XPM lets you run your legacy Windows XP applications inside a virtualized environment, either from within a virtual XP window or as a seamlessly integrated application within Windows 7.

A virtualized environment creates an environment that mimics an actual computer, so in XPM, you've got a copy of Windows XP that thinks it's got a computer all to itself. As a result, applications that run under XPM are similarly fooled: as far as they are concerned, they are running under Windows XP, and do not interact directly with Windows 7.

Installing Windows XP Mode

XPM is available for the following Windows 7 editions: Professional, Ultimate, and Enterprise. If you don't find it on your Start menu, you'll need to get two things: Windows Virtual PC and the Windows XP Mode package. If Windows Virtual PC is already installed, you can skip ahead to the Windows XP Mode package instructions.

To get Windows Virtual PC, head over to *http://www.microsoft.com/windows/virtual-pc/download.aspx* and download Windows Virtual PC. Windows Virtual PC is a small Windows update package (about 5 MB) that will install on your Windows 7 computer.

Windows Virtual PC is an enhanced, but slightly stripped-down, version of Microsoft Virtual PC 2007. This new version is especially designed for Windows 7 so that it can support the seamless XP Mode and USB devices.

Once Windows Virtual PC is downloaded, proceed with the installation. When the installation is completed, you may be prompted to restart your computer.

The next step is to download Windows XP Mode package. The Windows XP Mode package contains the hard disk image of an actual Windows XP installation (with Service Pack 3 applied). Be aware that the package takes up a whopping 445 MB of disk space, so you may want to start downloading it before you go to sleep.

In general, you need a separate license for each virtual operating system you install on your computer. In this case, you are essentially getting a free Windows XP license on your computer.

Once the package is downloaded, proceed with the installation. You will be asked to specify a password to use for the Virtual Windows XP .

If you check the "Remember credentials (Recommended)" checkbox, you won't need to log in again the next time you launch Virtual Windows XP. Instead, your credentials will be supplied to the virtual machine automatically.

You will then be asked a couple of questions. Basically, you are configuring another installation of Windows, so the steps are very similar to configuring a new computer.

The first time you launch it, Virtual Windows XP will set itself up for first-time use. This can take a bit of time (five minutes or more).

Using Windows XP Mode

When Windows XP Mode is ready, it will display the Virtual Windows XP window (see Figure 7-1). Essentially, this is an instance of Windows XP running in a virtual PC.

You can now install your legacy applications on this virtual Windows XP and run them within the window.

All your drives in your host computer (Windows 7) are accessible in the Virtual Windows XP. Your drive will be named after this format:

<Drive letter> on <Computer name>

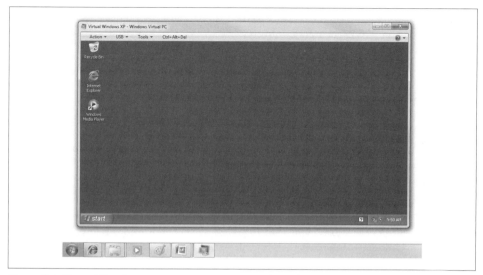

Figure 7-1. Virtual Windows XP running an instance of Windows XP

Figure 7-2 shows the drives on my Windows 7 computer mapped as network drives and visible in the Virtual Windows XP. This means that you can save your work either within the Virtual Windows XP or directly onto your Windows 7 drives.

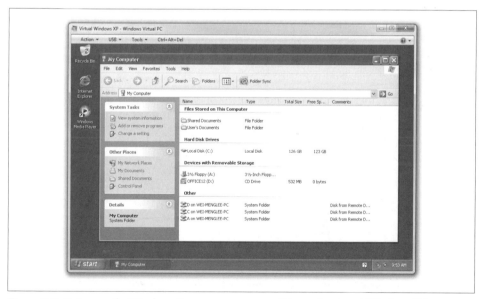

Figure 7-2. Drives on the Windows 7 computer are accessible on the virtual Windows XP

One annoying limitation of the Virtual Windows XP window is that you cannot drag-and-drop items between the host computer and itself (which is not the case for Virtual PC 2007).

Error Restarting Virtual Machines

Sometimes you may encounter problems restarting virtual machines that have been hibernating. For example, when I tried to restart my Virtual Windows XP after I hibernated it, I got the error message shown in Figure 7-3 that prevented me from starting the virtual machine.

To resolve this error, the easiest way would be to delete the corresponding *.vsv* file for the virtual machine so that it loses its previously saved state. In my case, the *Virtual Windows XP.vsv* file is located in *C:\Users\Wei-Meng Lee\AppData\Local\Microsoft \Windows Virtual PC\Virtual Machines* (see Figure 7-4; you need to enable the "Show hidden files, folders, and drives" option in Windows Explorer's options). Deleting the *.vsv* file is equivalent to pulling out the power plug of a machine and performing a power off.

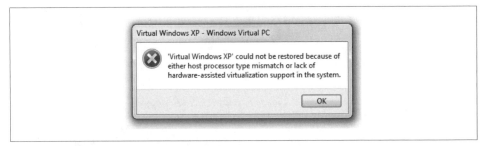

Figure 7-3. Problems starting Virtual Windows XP

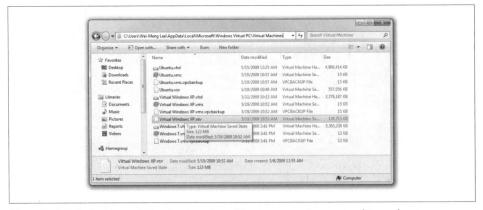

Figure 7-4. Deleting the .vsv file of a virtual machine to remove its previously saved state

Running Windows XP Mode Seamlessly with Windows 7

The coolest feature of Windows XP Mode is not its ability to run legacy applications on a virtual Windows XP window. Rather, it is that all applications you installed on the Virtual Windows XP are now available in the Start menu of your Windows 7 computer.

 Applications that you install onto the Virtual Windows XP will be visible in Windows 7 only if the applications you installed are for All Users. If you have accidentally installed an application for a specific user, you can move it to All Users pretty easily: right-click XP's Start menu and choose Explore All Users. Do this again, but choose "Explore." Find the application you installed and drag it to the corresponding location in the All Users Start menu.

Figure 7-5 shows my Start menu with a Windows Virtual PC item, which is expanded to show three more items.

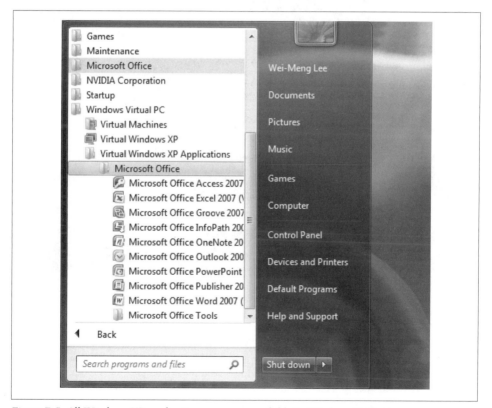

Figure 7-5. All Windows XP applications are now available in Windows 7's Start menu

Virtual Machines
Opens a window and shows the list of virtual machines available on your computer.

Virtual Windows XP
Launches the Virtual Windows XP window.

Virtual Windows XP Applications
Expands and displays the list of applications installed within the virtual Windows XP. This may not appear until you have installed some applications in the Virtual Windows XP.

As you can observe in Figure 7-5, I have installed Microsoft Office in Virtual Windows XP and the suite of applications is now available to me on Windows 7.

Figure 7-6 shows the Microsoft PowerPoint application running seamlessly within Windows 7.

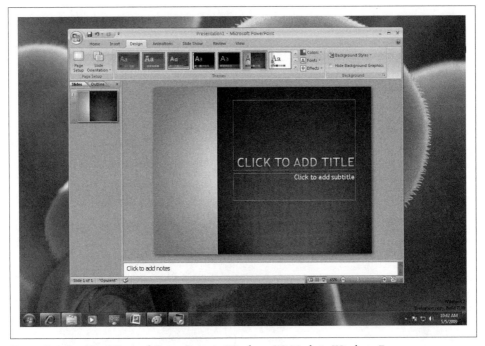

Figure 7-6. Running Microsoft PowerPoint in Windows XP Mode in Windows 7

 In order to run a Windows XP application in seamless mode, you should close the Virtual Windows XP window before you run the application. Otherwise, when you run a Windows XP application in seamless mode, it will offer to log off the user who is currently logged on in Virtual PC.

Similarly, if you want to launch the Virtual Windows XP window, all applications running in Windows XP Mode should be closed, too.

Note that applications running in Windows XP Mode use the default Windows XP theme. Figure 7-7 shows the themes used by the two PowerPoint applications: the background instance runs natively on Windows 7, while the foreground instance runs in Windows XP Mode.

Figure 7-7. The different themes used by native and Windows XP Mode applications

USB Mode

One of the most requested features of Virtual PC was support for USB devices. In Windows Virtual PC, users saw their dreams come true. Windows Virtual PC now comes with support for USB devices (see Figure 7-8).

When Virtual Windows XP is launched, it automatically scans for USB devices attached to your host Windows 7 computer. All USB devices will be displayed under the USB menu item. If you want to use them from within your Windows XP computer, simply select the item containing the device you want to use. The status of the device will then switch from Attach to Release. Virtual Windows XP will then proceed to look for the drivers for the selected device.

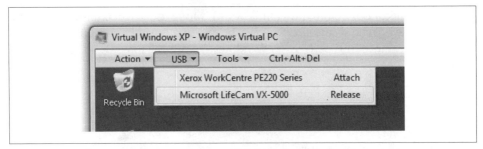

Figure 7-8. Windows Virtual PC now supports USB devices attached to the host computer

Installing Other Operating Systems

When you install Windows Virtual PC and the XPM package, you get the Windows XP virtual machine free of charge so that you can run your legacy Windows XP applications. However, besides running the free Windows XP virtual machine, you can also install other operating systems on Windows Virtual PC. This section will show you how to install another operating system on Windows Virtual PC. For illustration purposes, I will install the Ubuntu Linux OS.

Creating a New Virtual Machine

First, launch the Virtual Machines window by going to Start→All Programs→Windows Virtual PC→Virtual Machines. The Virtual Machines window will be shown (see Figure 7-9). This window will display all the virtual machines that you have installed on your computer.

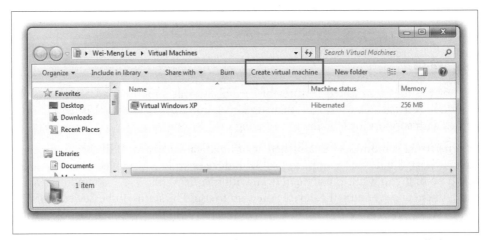

Figure 7-9. The Virtual Machines window, displaying the virtual machines you have installed on your computer

To create a new virtual machine, click the menu item "Create virtual machine." You will be asked to name the new virtual machine as well as specify a location to store the new virtual machine file. Click Next.

In the next screen, you need to specify how much memory to allocate to this virtual machine. You will also indicate whether you want the virtual machine to make use of the current computer's network connection for network access. Click Next to continue.

Finally, you will be asked to create or use an existing hard disk image file for the new OS. If you are creating a new image, select the first option and click Create.

Starting the New Virtual Machine

Once the virtual machine is created, you will see it shown in the Virtual Machines window (see Figure 7-10).

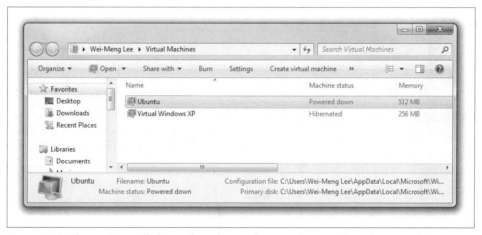

Figure 7-10. The newly installed virtual machine is shown in the Virtual Machines window

To start the new virtual machine, double-click it. The virtual machine will attempt to perform a network boot, and will eventually fail. As you have not installed the OS yet, press the Esc key now and you will see a message asking you to reboot or insert the boot media in the selected boot device.

To install an OS on the virtual machine, you will need the installation disc for the OS you are going to install and you must let Windows Virtual PC know how to locate the installation disc. To do so, select Tools→Settings... and choose DVD Drive from the list of settings.

If your OS comes on a physical disc, insert the disc (CD or DVD) into your CD/DVD drive now and select the "Access a physical drive option" (Figure 7-11). Choose the drive letter that corresponds to your disc drive. If your OS is saved as an ISO file, choose the "Open an ISO image" option and specify the path containing the ISO file. Click OK to continue.

Figure 7-11. Mapping the DVD drive

Click the menu labeled Ctrl-Alt-Del in the virtual machine window. The virtual machine will now attempt to boot up. If the bootup is successful, you should see a bootup screen like Figure 7-12.

You will now proceed with the usual steps to install the OS. Figure 7-13 shows my newly installed Ubuntu running in Windows Virtual PC.

Figure 7-12. Successfully booting up the OS

Figure 7-13. The Ubuntu OS running in Windows Virtual PC

Summary

In this chapter, you have seen the new Windows XP Mode (XPM) available in Windows 7. XPM is a good solution for users who are still using legacy Windows XP applications to move to Windows 7 without needing to worry whether their old applications are still supported. Though most Windows XP and Vista applications should run without any problems in Windows 7, XPM will serve as a good backup to ensure the maximum support for all applications.

CHAPTER 8

Windows 7 Tips and Tricks

Windows 7 is a complex operating system that is more evolutionary than revolutionary. A lot of features available in Windows 7 are based on the features available in the earlier versions of Windows—XP and Vista. Nevertheless, Windows 7 contains a wealth of new features that greatly improve the usability of Windows and its performance. In this chapter, you will learn some of the tips and tricks to getting the most out of Windows 7.

Customizing the UI

In Windows 7, Windows Explorer has gone though a kind facelift, evident most notably in the new Libraries feature, as well as with native support for touchscreens. Apart from this, Windows 7 also packs some nice little surprises to spice up your Windows experience.

Change Windows Explorer's Default View

When you launch Windows Explorer, the default view you will get is always the Libraries (see Figure 8-1).

Though Microsoft thinks that your interaction with files should center around Libraries, not everyone will find it useful. In particular, you may want Computer (where it will display the disk drives available on your computer) to be displayed when you open Windows Explorer.

To display something different, such as Computer, when you open Windows Explorer, you need to undertake some tweaks. Click the Start menu and select All Programs→Accessories. Right-click the Windows Explorer icon and select Properties (see Figure 8-2).

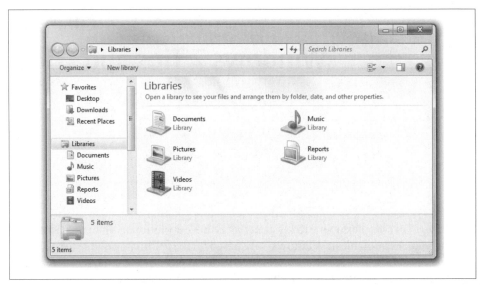

Figure 8-1. The default view of Windows Explorer

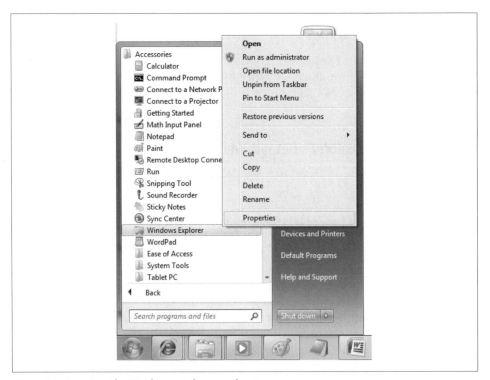

Figure 8-2. Locating the Windows Explorer application

In the Properties window, click the Shortcut tab; you should see the Target attribute set to:

```
%windir%\explorer.exe
```

Change it to the following (see also Figure 8-3):

```
%SystemRoot%\explorer.exe /root,::{20D04FE0-3AEA-1069-A2D8-08002B30309D}
```

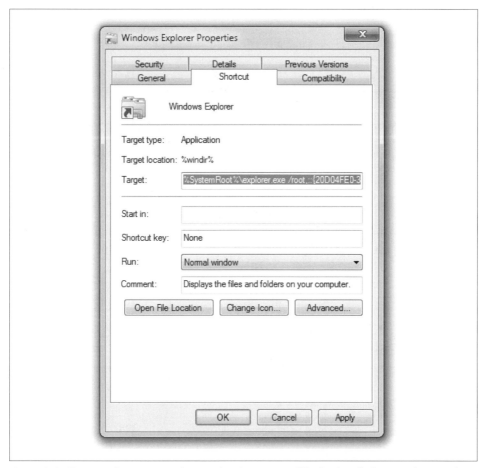

Figure 8-3. Changing the Target attribute so that Computer will be displayed when Windows Explorer is opened

Once this step is performed, whenever you open Windows Explorer, Computer will now be shown (see Figure 8-4).

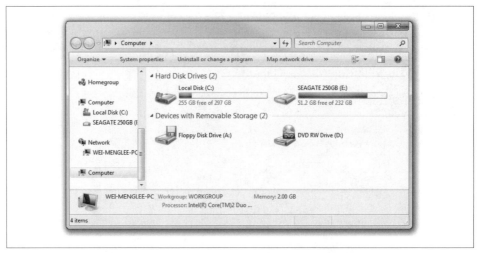

Figure 8-4. Displaying Computer when Windows Explorer is opened

Note that performing the steps outlined here affects Windows Explorer only in the Accessories folder. That is, if you launch Windows Explorer from the icon pinned to the taskbar, you will still see the Libraries. To fix this, you need to unpin the Windows Explorer icon from the taskbar (see Figure 8-5) and then pin it to the taskbar again.

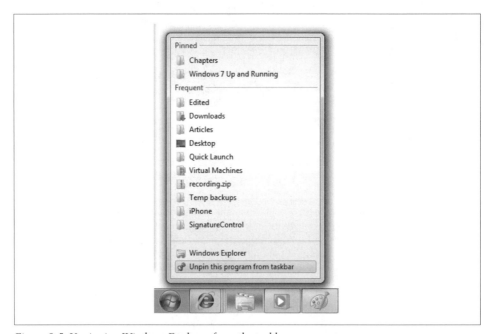

Figure 8-5. Unpinning Windows Explorer from the taskbar

Note that if you right-click the Start menu and select Windows Explorer, it will still display the Libraries.

Open a Command Window Anywhere

If you are used to the command line, you will appreciate this tip. In Windows 7, you can use Windows Explorer to navigate to any folder you want and then Shift-right-click a folder and select the "Open command window here" option (see Figure 8-6).

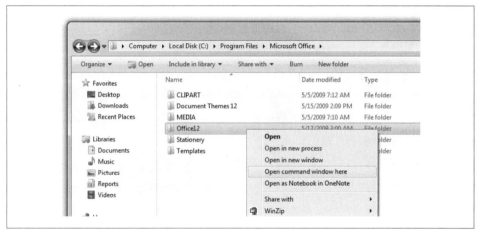

Figure 8-6. Shift-right-click a folder to open a command window

Doing so will open a command window at the selected folder (see Figure 8-7).

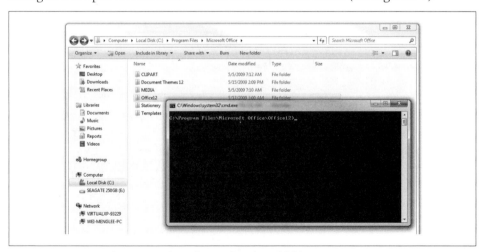

Figure 8-7. Opening the command window at the selected folder

Use Themes for Other Locations

When you install Windows 7, you are asked to select your current location. The location that you select will determine the themes that you will see in Control Panel (under the Personalization application).

For example, if you have selected United States for your location, you should see the Aero Themes, as shown in Figure 8-8.

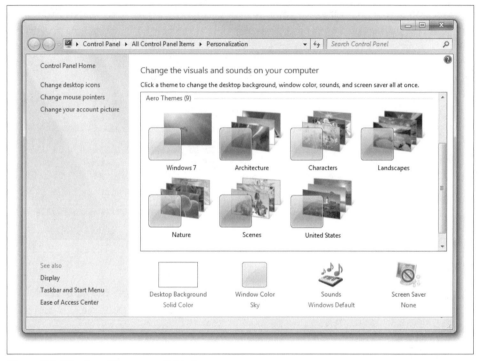

Figure 8-8. The Aero Themes available for your computer

However, if you now change your location to some other place, such as Canada or United Kingdom, your Personalization control panel will now include themes for these additional locations. Figure 8-9 shows the additional themes that were added to the Personalization application when I changed my location to Canada and then the United Kingdom.

If you change to a location that Windows does not have a theme for (such as France), you will not see any changes to the Personalization control panel. You can go online and download additional themes, though.

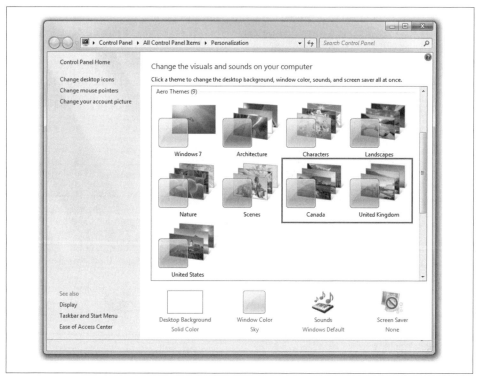

Figure 8-9. The additional themes added

Besides changing your location to see the additional themes available, you can also go to a hidden folder (*C:\Windows\Globalization\MCT*) to locate the additional themes (see Figure 8-10).

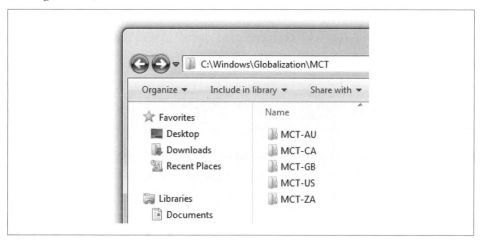

Figure 8-10. Additional themes in the hidden folder

As you can see, there are five folders, each representing a location—Australia (MCT-AU), Canada (MCT-CA), United Kingdom (MCT-GB), United States (MCT-US), and South Africa (MCT-ZA). Within each folder are several subfolders, one of which is the *Theme* folder. Inside the *Theme* folder, you will see a *.theme* file. When you double-click the *.theme* file, the current theme will be changed to the selected theme, and it will also appear in the My Themes section of the Personalization application (see Figure 8-11).

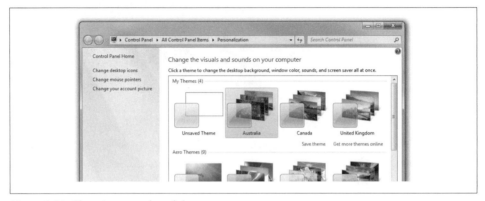

Figure 8-11. Changing to a selected theme

Touch Gestures

Windows 7 is designed with touchscreen support, and hence some of the UI elements in Windows have implicit support for hand gestures, even if you don't have hardware support for touch. For example, in IE, you can use your mouse and click and drag down the Address bar. IE will slide the history and favorites list into view as you drag (see Figure 8-12).

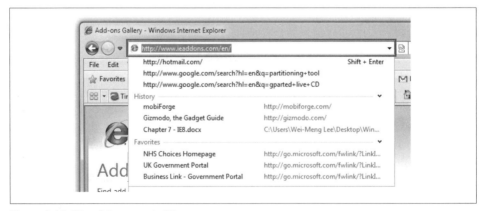

Figure 8-12. "Touch" support in IE

Of course, if you have a touch-enabled screen, the easiest way would be to use your finger and swipe the Address bar downward.

The taskbar also supports touch; use your mouse and click an application icon in the taskbar and move upward; it will fade and slide the Jump List into view (see Figure 8-13).

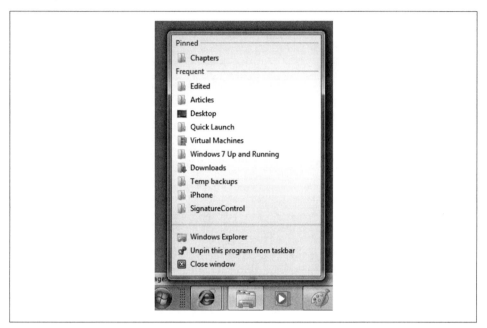

Figure 8-13. Swiping an application icon upward displays the Jump Lists

Auto-Login

In Windows 7, you can use the Advanced User Account feature to automatically log in with your user account whenever you boot up your computer.

To use the Advanced User Account feature, click the Start menu, type "netplwiz" in the search box, and press Return. The User Accounts window will appear (see Figure 8-14).

 The Advanced User Account feature is also accessible with the command `control userpasswords2`, but it must be typed at the command prompt or Run (Windows-R) dialog.

Figure 8-14. The User Accounts window to configure user access to your computer

Select the user to use to auto-login and then uncheck the "Users must enter a user name and password to use this computer" checkbox. You will be asked to enter the password twice.

Now when you start up your computer, you will be automatically logged in.

Taskbar

The new taskbar is one of the highlights in Windows 7. It is greatly improved, but is still one of the areas that you can tweak to your heart's content.

Rearranging the Icons in the Taskbar

In the previous versions of Windows, icons displayed in the taskbar are static; that is, you cannot move them. In Windows 7, you can freely move the icons anywhere in the taskbar simply by dragging-and-dropping them within the taskbar (see Figure 8-15).

Figure 8-15. Rearrange the icons in the taskbar by dragging-and-dropping them on the desired location

Displaying the Old Quick Launch Bar

Despite the many improvements made to the taskbar in Windows 7, some users may still miss the old Quick Launch bar available in Windows XP and Vista. Follow these steps to get the Quick Launch bar back to the taskbar:

1. Right-click the taskbar and uncheck the "Lock the taskbar" option.
2. Right-click the taskbar and select Toolbars→New Toolbar.
3. When asked to choose a folder, enter the following (see Figure 8-16) and then click the Select Folder button:

        %userprofile%\AppData\Roaming\Microsoft\Internet Explorer\Quick Launch

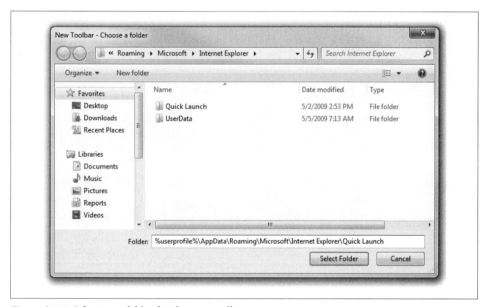

Figure 8-16. Selecting a folder for the new toolbar

The Quick Launch bar will now appear at the right side of the taskbar (see Figure 8-17).

Figure 8-17. The Quick Launch bar

Click the divider and drag Quick Launch bar to reveal the items contained within it (see Figure 8-18).

Figure 8-18. Exposing the items contained within the Quick Launch bar

Taskbar Shortcuts

The taskbar contains many shortcuts that will make your life much easier. Here are some really helpful ones:

Ctrl-click an application icon in the taskbar
    This action will cycle through all the open windows belonging to the application. For example, suppose that you have five IE windows open. Pressing the Ctrl key while you click the IE icon in the taskbar will toggle between all the opened IE windows (including tab pages).

Shift-click (or middle-click) an application icon in the taskbar
    This will launch a new instance of the application.

Ctrl-Shift-Click an application icon in the taskbar
    This action will launch the application in administrator mode.

Besides these taskbar shortcuts, the Windows Key has many shortcuts as well. Table 8-1 shows the various shortcuts you can use with the Windows Key.

Table 8-1. Windows Key shortcuts

Key combinations	Descriptions
Windows Key + ↓	Minimizes/restores window
Windows Key + ←	Docks window to left of screen

Key combinations	Descriptions
Windows Key + →	Docks window to right of screen
Windows Key + ↑	Maximizes window
Windows Key + −	Zooms out when magnifier is active
Windows Key + +	Activates magnifier and zoom in
Windows Key + B	Switches focus to the notification area (use arrow keys to navigate)
Windows Key + D	Shows the desktop
Windows Key + E	Opens Windows Explorer
Windows Key + F	Opens the search Window
Windows Key + G	Cycles through the Gadgets
Windows Key + Home	Minimizes/restores all other windows
Windows Key + L	Locks the screen
Windows Key + M	Minimizes all windows
Windows Key + *n*	Opens or launches the application located on the corresponding position in the taskbar (starting with 1 from the left, not counting the Start menu); if the application is not running, it launches it; otherwise, it displays the window list while you hold down the key, and activates the first item in the list
Windows Key + P	Shows the display options pop up
Windows Key + R	Shows the Run dialog
Windows Key + T	Cycles through all the icons in the taskbar from left to right
Windows Key + U	Opens the Ease of Access Center
Windows Key + X	Launches Windows Mobility Center (on notebooks and mobile computers)
Windows Key + Shift + ←	Moves to left monitor
Windows Key + Shift + →	Moves to right monitor
Windows Key + Shift + T	Cycles through all the icons in the taskbar from right to left
Windows Key + Space	Peeks at the desktop

Another useful shortcut is Alt-P, which shows the File Preview Pane in Windows Explorer. Figure 8-19 shows the File Preview Pane displaying the preview of a selected image when you press the Alt-P shortcut.

Besides using the File Preview Pane to preview images, you can also use it to preview known file types such as Word (see Figure 8-20) and PowerPoint documents.

Figure 8-19. The File Preview Pane in Windows Explorer

Figure 8-20. Previewing a Word document

Pinning Folders to the Taskbar

If you frequently work with certain folders, you might want to pin them to the taskbar. To pin a folder to the taskbar, drag-and-drop it onto the taskbar (see Figure 8-21). The folder will now appear in the Pinned section of the Windows Explorer Jump List.

Figure 8-21. Pinning a folder to the taskbar

Utilities/Troubleshooting Tools

Windows 7 ships with some really neat utilities to help you work with external accessories as well as troubleshoot problems. Here are some of the cool ones.

Projector Screen Selection

If you have ever done presentations using your notebook computer, you know the kind of nightmare you sometimes have to go through to get your display projected correctly on the projector screen—find the right key combinations on your keyboard, toggle a couple of times, and so on. If you want to use the projector screen as an extension of your screen, you need to go to the screen settings and mess with the setup again.

In Windows 7, you can now quickly control the display projection by pressing the Windows-P key combination. You will see the pop up shown in Figure 8-22.

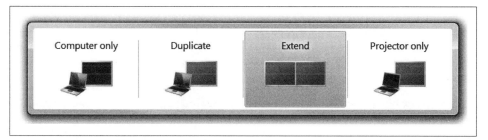

Figure 8-22. Controlling the display output options

As you can see, you can easily control how the display is shown on your computer and the projector simply by selecting the option that applies to you.

 You can also use the command `displayswitch.exe` to invoke the projector pop up. You can run it from the command prompt or the search field of the Start menu.

Problems Steps Recorder

One very cool tool shipped in Windows 7 is the Problems Steps Recorder application. This is one of the internal tools that Microsoft uses for feedback, now available in Windows 7. The Problems Steps Recorder application basically captures screenshots of what you are doing and details each step with descriptions of the actions that you performed. When you are done recording, the details are saved as a web archive.

To launch the Problems Steps Recorder application, use the command `psr.exe` (you can also find it by searching for "Record steps to reproduce a problem" in the Control Panel). When the application is launched, you will see the window shown in Figure 8-23.

Figure 8-23. The Problem Steps Recorder

To start recording, click the Start Record button. From this point onward, whatever items you click on the desktop will be recorded. In the process, you can also add your own comments (in addition, the system will automatically insert detailed descriptions of what you are doing). When you are done, click the Stop Record button. You will now be asked to specify a filename for saving the recording.

The recording will be saved as a *.mht* file (archived web page) and zipped automatically to save space.

Open the archived report and you will see a detailed description of what you did (see Figure 8-24).

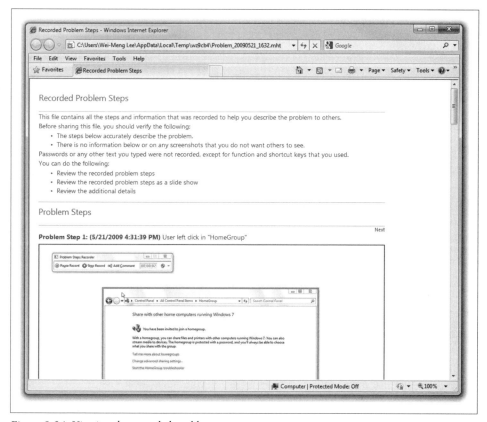

Figure 8-24. Viewing the recorded problem steps

The entire Windows desktop is captured in the report.

You can also view the report as a slideshow. Click the "Review the recorded problem steps as a slide show" link. Figure 8-25 shows the report as a slideshow.

Troubleshooting Sleep Mode Problems

If you use Windows 7 for some time, you may realize that your computer will suddenly wake up from sleep mode, or that the battery of your notebook computer drains very quickly. The possible causes of these symptoms are many and are often difficult to troubleshoot.

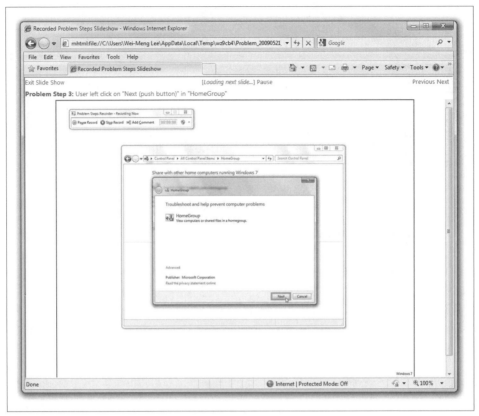

Figure 8-25. Viewing the recordings as a slideshow

Windows 7 includes a very useful tool to troubleshoot potential problems with your computer that may cause unexpected drain on the battery of your notebook. It can also troubleshoot areas that cause problems with sleep modes, and display the different power saving modes supported by your computer. To launch this tool, launch the command window in Administrator mode (type **cmd.exe** in the Start menu, right-click the **cmd.exe** item, and select "Run as administrator").

Then, type the following command:

```
powercfg -energy
```

 You can also use the *powercfg* tool to turn off hibernation (you need to run the command as an Administrator):

```
powercfg -h off
```

The *Power Policy Configuration* tool will take a while to complete; when it is done, you will see the information displayed as follows:

```
C:\Windows\system32>powercfg -energy
Enabling tracing for 60 seconds...
Observing system behavior...
Analyzing trace data...
Analysis complete.

Energy efficiency problems were found.

9 Errors
14 Warnings
10 Informational

See C:\Windows\system32\energy-report.html for more details.
```

The report generated is named *energy-report.html* and is saved in your current working directory. You can navigate to the folder and use IE8 to view its content (see Figure 8-26).

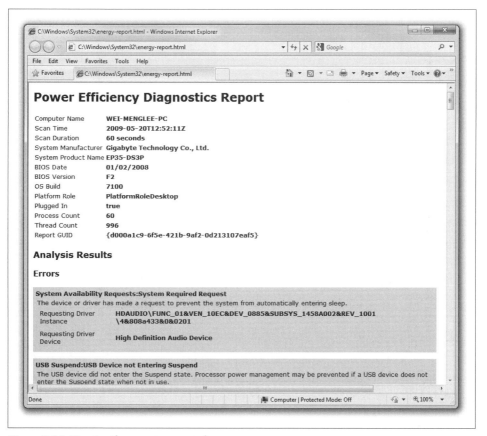

Figure 8-26. Viewing the report generated

Instead of navigating to the destination folder to view the report, you can issue the following command in the command window to launch the report directly:

```
start energy-report.html
```

You need to run this from the command window from which you ran `powercfg`; otherwise, you may not be in the correct directory.

Windows Disk Image Burner

In previous versions of Windows, you needed a third-party application to burn an ISO image to your CD or DVD. In Windows 7, this capability is built right into the OS. By default, you can double-click an ISO image and Windows will display the prompt shown in Figure 8-27.

Figure 8-27. The Windows Disc Image Burner

Select the CD/DVD burner, insert a disc, and click the Burn button to start burning your CD/DVD.

Calibrating Your Display

Windows 7 includes two cool tools to calibrate your display for text and graphics. These tools are especially useful for notebook computer screens, as they make your display much sharper. These two tools can be launched using Control Pane→Appearance and Personalization→Display.

 The two tools can also be launched via the command line—cttune.exe and dccw.exe.

The *cttune.exe* application (the "Adjust ClearType text" link on the left of the window) helps you to calibrate your display for displaying ClearType text (see Figure 8-28).

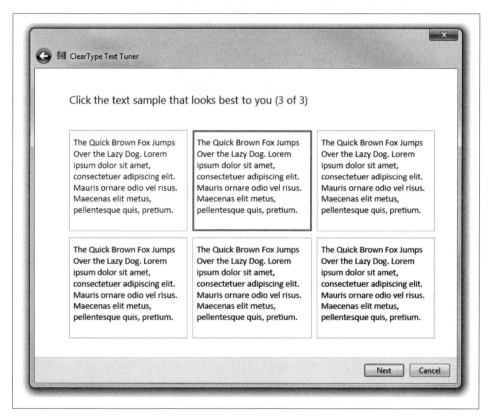

Figure 8-28. The cttune application

The *dccw.exe* application (the "Calibrate color" link) helps you to calibrate the color of your display so that colors can appear accurately (see Figure 8-29).

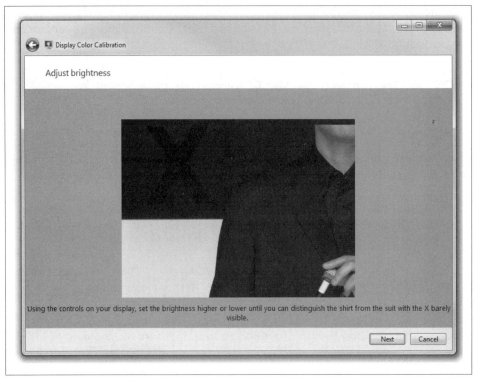

Figure 8-29. The dccw application

Windows 7 Compatibility Mode

If you have trouble running applications designed for the previous versions of Windows, you can also use the Windows 7 Compatibility Mode to run them in Windows 7. Using the Compatibility Mode, you can configure an application to try to run in the version of Windows that it was written for.

To configure an application to run in Compatibility Mode, right-click the application's shortcut, *.exe*, or installation program, and select Properties. Next, select the Compatibility tab and you should see the option "Run this program in compatibility mode for:" (see Figure 8-30).

Note that if Compatibility Mode is not supported for the application, the option will appear grayed out. The most likely reasons for this are that the application is designed for Windows 7 only, or that it is a 64-bit application.

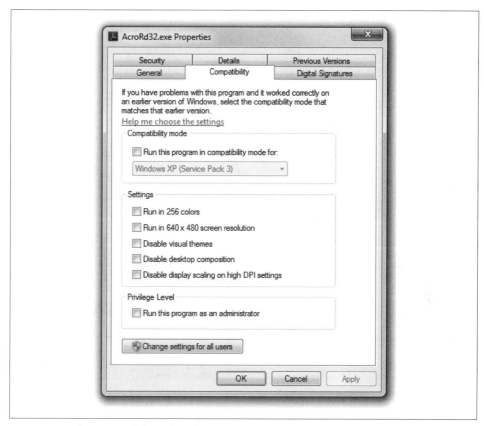

Figure 8-30. The Compatibility tab in the Properties window

Check the option and you will be able to select the versions of Windows to use to run the application (see Figure 8-31).

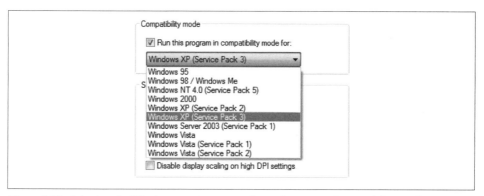

Figure 8-31. Selecting the Windows version to run the application in Compatibility Mode

Do not use Compatibility Mode for antivirus programs and disk utilities, as this may cause data loss.

You will also be able to modify various other settings such as colors, resolutions, themes, desktop composition (disabling this turns off Aero effects), and DPI settings. You will also be able to run the application as an administrator.

If you are not sure which are the best settings to use, you can use the Program Compatibility application shipped with Windows 7. To invoke the Program Compatibility application, type the following command in the command window or the Run dialog (see Figure 8-32):

```
msdt -id PCWDiagnostic
```

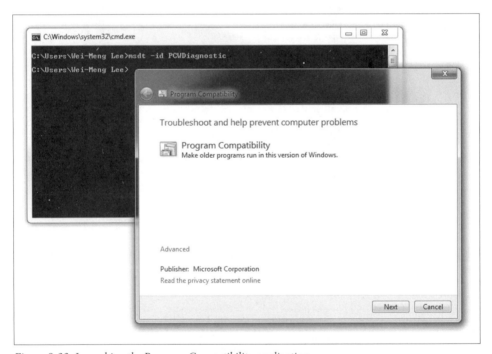

Figure 8-32. Launching the Program Compatibility application

 The Program Compatibility application can also be launched from Control Panel→Programs→Run Programs made for previous versions of Windows.

Follow through the wizard and it will guide you and provide recommendations for the settings to use.

Installing Windows 7

Netbooks are all the rage nowadays, with manufacturers rolling out new netbooks at an incredible rate. Windows 7 is a popular choice for installing on netbooks, as it is designed and optimized for low-powered computers like netbooks. However, one limitation of netbooks is that they do not have DVD drives, and this makes installing a new OS on them a bit challenging. Fear not: armed with a computer running Vista or Windows 7 and a USB hard disk or thumb drive, you can install Windows 7 on a netbook easily. Here's how.

Installing Windows 7 Using a USB Hard Drive

You can install Windows 7 using a USB hard drive. The following steps show you how to prepare your existing USB hard drive for installing Windows 7:

1. Connect your USB hard disk to your computer.
2. Launch the Disk Management application available in Windows.

> In Windows Vista, the Disk Management tool is found under Control Panel→Administrative Tools→Computer Management. In Windows 7, type "disk management" in the Start menu to launch it.

3. Locate the USB hard drive and right-click it (see Figure 8-33). Select Shrink Volume....

Figure 8-33. Shrinking an existing hard disk

4. You will be asked the size in MB to shrink. Enter an amount greater than 3,000 (3 GB). For my example, I used 15,000 (15 GB; see Figure 8-34). Click Shrink.

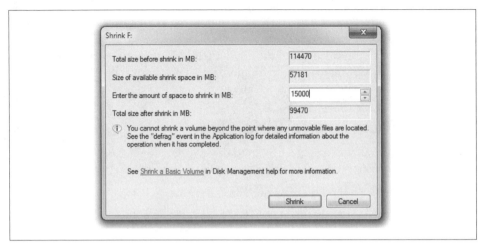

Figure 8-34. Specifying the amount to shrink

5. When the shrinking is done, right-click the new partition and select New Simple Volume (see Figure 8-35).

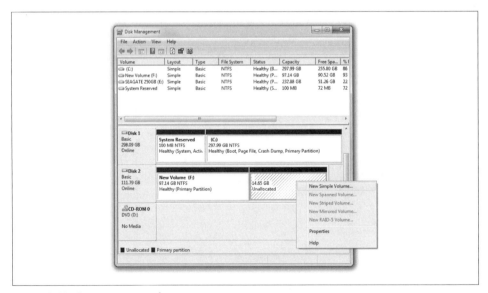

Figure 8-35. Creating a new volume

6. The New Simple Volume wizard will appear. Click Next.

7. Specify the size for the new volume: 15,000. Click Next.

8. Assign a new drive letter—use the default drive letter assigned. Click Next.

9. Format the drive using FAT32 (see Figure 8-36). Click Next.

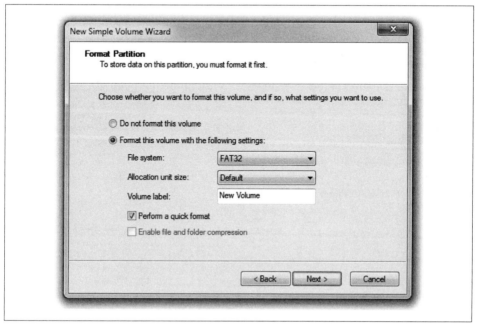

Figure 8-36. Formatting the drive using FAT32

10. To complete the wizard, click Finish.

11. Right-click the new partition and select Mark Partition as Active to make it as the bootable partition (see Figure 8-37).

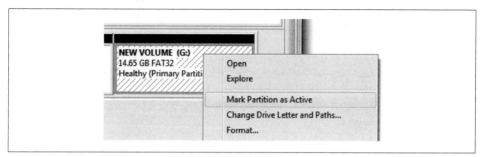

Figure 8-37. Marking the partition as bootable

12. Copy all the files from the Windows 7 installation disk onto the newly created drive.

13. If your Windows 7 comes as an ISO image, you can download third-party applications to mount the ISO image as a DVD drive. The application I used is Virtual CloneDrive. You can download the free Virtual CloneDrive from *http://www.sly soft.com/en/download.html*.

You can now connect the USB hard disk to your computer and boot from the USB drive (during bootup, you need to instruct the BIOS to boot up using your USB devices).

Installing Windows 7 Using a USB Thumb Drive

If you want to install Windows 7 using a USB thumb drive, follow the steps outlined here:

1. Use the *diskpart.exe* application to prepare the USB thumb drive. Launch the *diskpart.exe* application in the command prompt and then issue the following commands (see also Figure 8-38):

```
list disk
select disk n (where n is your thumb drive)
clean
create partition primary
format fs=fat32 quick
active
exit
```

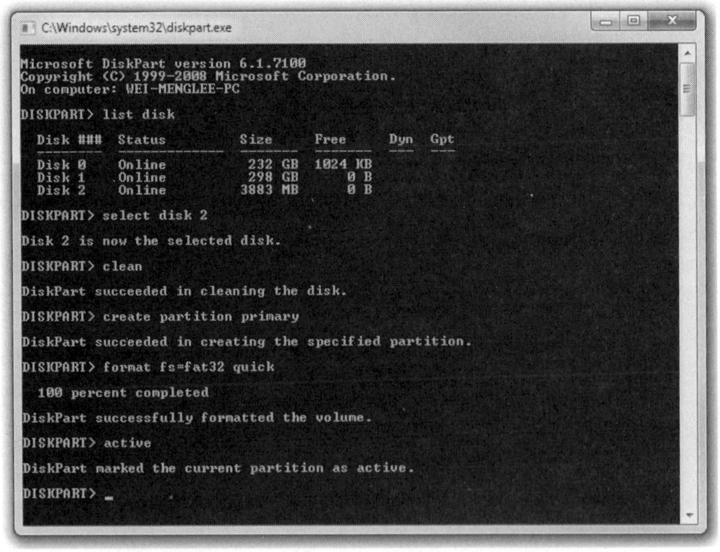

Figure 8-38. Preparing the thumb drive with diskpart.exe

2. Copy the content of the Windows 7 installation disk onto the USB thumb drive.

3. Insert the thumb drive into the computer and boot it up using the USB thumb drive.

 As the Windows 7 installation takes up well over 2 GB, you would need a USB thumb drive that is at least 4 GB.

Dual Booting Windows 7 with Windows Vista and Windows XP

Although Windows 7 offers many features and performance enhancements, you might not be ready to totally move to this new operating system. In this case, a good solution would be to keep your existing OS (XP or Vista) and install Windows 7 as a dual-boot system. Installing Windows 7 as a dual-boot system requires disk partitioning, and this section shows you how.

 Before you proceed with preparing your existing hard disk for a dual boot, be sure to back up your existing files. Partitioning a hard disk is like walking a tightrope—you never know when an accident will occur.

If you are currently running Windows XP, you need to use some third-party partitioning software, such as Partition Magic (*http://www.symantec.com/norton/partitionmagic*) or GParted (*http://gparted.sourceforge.net*). The key here is to resize your current partition and create a new partition of at least 16 GB. In Vista, you can use the Disk Management tool (Control Panel→Administrative Tools→Computer Management) to shrink the existing hard disk (see Figure 8-39) to create a new partition of at least 16 GB. Once the disk has been shrunken, create a new simple volume on the free space.

Figure 8-39. Shrinking the partition in Windows Vista

Go back to the section "Installing Windows 7 Using a USB Hard Drive" on page 167 to learn how to use the Disk Management tool.

Reboot the computer using the Windows 7 disk (or USB thumb drive or hard disk). During the installation, select Custom (advanced) when asked to choose the installation type and choose the newly created partition to set up Windows 7.

When the installation is done, you will have a dual-boot system that allows you to select the OS to boot when you start up your computer.

Installing Windows 7 on a Virtual Hard Disk (VHD) File

Virtual machine technologies have been around for quite some time, and Microsoft is a strong proponent of this technology, with products like Virtual PC and Virtual Server. Using virtual machines, the operating system is installed on a virtual hard disk and the operating system runs on an emulated hardware environment. However, the key limitation of virtual machines is that they cannot leverage all the hardware available on the system, such as graphics, wireless, USB, and so on.

In Windows 7, the Virtual Hard Disk that is used by Virtual PC (and other virtualization products) is now natively supported. This means that you can now install the entire operating system on a single VHD file and boot the computer off the single VHD file. This allows the operating system to run natively on the hardware (and not on emulation) and makes it very easy for administrators and developers to test different configurations of systems.

The following steps will show you how to install Windows 7 on a VHD file using a new fresh hard disk:

1. Using the Windows installation disk, boot up your computer.
2. When you are asked to select a language, select the appropriate language.
3. Press Shift-F10 to launch a command console window (see Figure 8-40).
4. In the command window, issue the following commands (replace 60,000 with the maximum size, in megabytes, for the VHD image):
    a. `diskpart`
    b. `list disk`
    c. `sel disk 0`
    d. `create partition primary`
    e. `format fs=ntfs quick`
    f. `list vol`
    g. `assign`

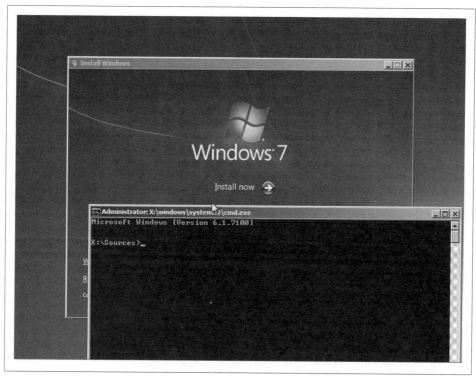

Figure 8-40. Launching a command window during installation time

    h. `list vol`

    i. `create vdisk file=C:\Windows7.vhd maximum=60000 type=expandable`

    j. `select vdisk file=C:\Windows7.vhd`

    k. `attach vdisk`

    l. `create partition primary`

    m. `format fs=ntfs quick`

    n. `assign letter=U:`

    o. `list vol`

    p. `list vdisk`

    q. `exit diskpart`

    r. `exit`

5. These commands first create a primary partition on your hard disk and then create a new VHD file (of size 60 GB) in the primary partition.

6. Continue with the installation of Windows 7. You will now have created a VHD file on your drive, which looks like a normal partition to the Windows 7 installer

(see Figure 8-41). Select Disk 1 Partition 1 to install Windows 7 (ignore the error message displayed at the bottom of the window). Click Next.

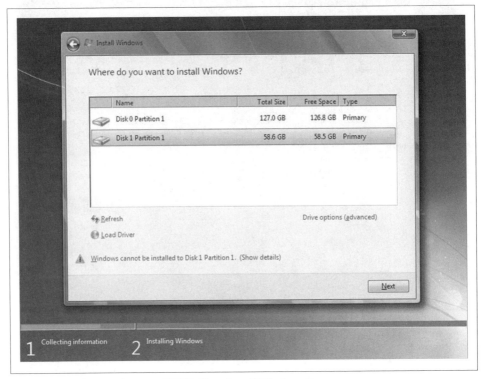

Figure 8-41. Selecting the created VHD file to install Windows 7

7. Following the instructions on the screen to complete the installation of Windows 7.

When Windows 7 is installed on the computer's hard disk, you can now proceed to install another operating system on the hard disk using a VHD file. The following steps show how to install another copy of the Windows 7 operating system using a VHD file:

1. Insert the Windows 7 DVD and boot up the computer using the DVD.

2. As in the previous list, press Shift-F10 after selecting the language to display the command window.

3. In the command window, issue the following commands:

    a. `create vdisk file=C:\newWindows7.vhd maximum=60000 type=expandable`

    b. `select vdisk file=C:\newWindows7.vhd`

    c. `attach vdisk`

    d. `exit`

4. These commands create another VHD file (also of size 60 GB) in the primary partition of your drive.

5. Exit the command prompt. Proceed to install Windows 7 as normal.

6. Once the installation is done, you will see two copies of Windows 7 in the boot loader when the computer restarts (see Figure 8-42). Select an instance to boot up.

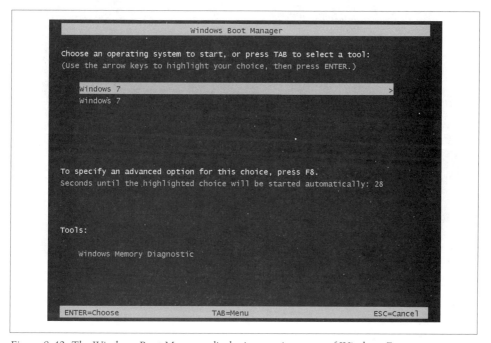

Figure 8-42. The Windows Boot Manager displaying two instances of Windows 7

7. To change the description of each Windows instance, run the command prompt window as an Administrator.

8. In the command window, type bcdedit /v. This will display the entries in the boot manager (see Figure 8-43). Observe the identifiers of each boot entry (those enclosed by the {}).

9. Enter the following command to change the description of the each entry in the boot manager (where {xxx} is the identifier of the boot entry you want to change):

```
bcdedit /set {xxxxxxxx-xxxx-xxxx-xxxx-xxxxxxxxxxxx} description "Windows 7 VHD"
```

10. Restart the computer; you should now see the updated description of each boot entries (see Figure 8-44).

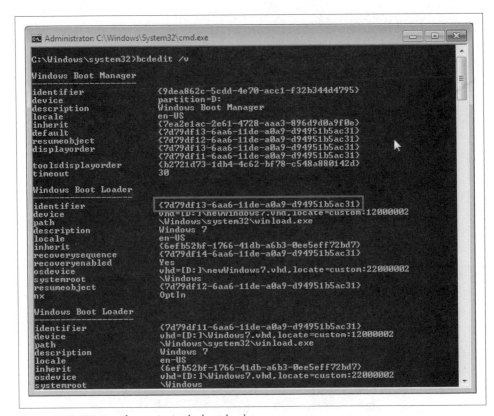

Figure 8-43. Viewing the entries in the boot loader

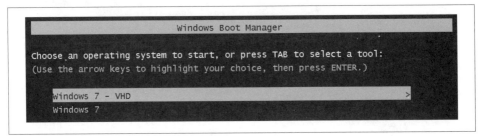

Figure 8-44. The boot loader with the updated entries

Summary

In this chapter, you have learned the many tips and tricks that allow you to customize Windows 7 to work the way you want. In particular, you have seen how to:

- Customize Windows Explorer and the taskbar, and apply themes to your Windows desktop
- Use the various keyboard shortcuts in Windows 7
- Use the various troubleshooting utilities in Windows 7 to troubleshoot Windows problems
- Burn ISO images to DVDs
- Use the touch gesture support in Windows 7
- Install Windows 7 using removable media such as USB thumb drives
- Dual-boot Windows 7 with Vista and Windows XP

Index

A

accelerators
  IE8, 120
Action Center, 53–55
Address bar
  IE8, 110
Advanced User Account feature
  auto-login, 151
Aero Peek
  about, 13
  taskbar, 20
Aero Shake, 14
Aero Snap, 14
antispyware
  Windows Defender, 73
antivirus tools
  AVG Anti-Virus, 76
  Compatibility Mode, 166
applications, 79–108
  Calculator, 16, 105
  Compatibility Mode, 164
  cttune.exe application, 163
  dccw.exe application, 164
  diskpart.exe application, 170
  displayswitch.exe command, 158
  legacy applications, 132, 135
  Math Input Panel, 103
  Microsoft Surface, 11
  Paint, 15, 107
  pinning to taskbar, 21
  powercfg tool, 160
  Snipping Tool, 92
  Sound Recorder, 94
  Sticky Notes, 105

  Windows Disc Image Burner, 99
  Windows Live Family Safety, 89
  Windows Live Mail, 81–87
  Windows Live Messenger, 80
  Windows Live Movie Maker, 91
  Windows Live Photo Gallery, 87
  Windows Live Writer, 88
  Windows Media Center, 101
  Windows Media Player, 107
  Windows Photo Viewer, 97
  Windows PowerShell, 95–97
  WordPad, 15, 107
  XPS Viewer, 104
auto-login, 151
AVG Anti-Virus, 76

B

back up
  certificates, 70
  Credential Manager, 63
BitLocker Drive Encryption, 64–68
BitLocker To Go, 67
blog publishing
  Windows Live Writer, 88
browsing
  tabbed in IE8, 110
burning
  DVDs, 98
  ISO and IMG images, 99

C

Calculator, 16, 105
Calendar, 84–87
calibrating

We'd like to hear your suggestions for improving our indexes. Send email to *index@oreilly.com*.

displays, 163
CDs
  burning, 99, 162
certificates
  back up, 70
  creating, 71
  importing, 73
command line
  opening command window, 147
  Windows PowerShell, 95–97
command prompt
  Windows PowerShell, 95
Compatibility View
  IE8, 112
Credential Manager, 59–64
  about, 60
  back up, 63
  linking online IDs, 61
credentials
  Virtual Windows XP, 132
Cross Site Scripting (XSS) Filter, 129
cttune.exe application, 163

D

dccw.exe application, 164
default view
  Windows Explorer, 143
destinations
  Jump Lists, 23
dir command
  Windows PowerShell, 95
Disc Image Burner, 99
disk images
  burning, 162
disk utilities
  Compatibility Mode, 166
diskpart.exe application, 170
displays
  calibrating, 163
displayswitch.exe command, 158
Dock feature
  Mac OS X, 21
domain highlighting
  IE8, 127
downloading
  Windows Live Essentials, 80
  XPM package, 132
drag-and-drop

between Virtual Windows XP and Windows
    7, 134
dragging windows, 14
drives
  using with Virtual Windows XP, 132
dual booting
  Windows 7 with Vista and XP, 171–172
DVDs
  burning, 98, 99, 162

E

editions of Windows 7
  list of, 1–3
  NTFS encryption availability, 69
  Windows Media Center, 101
  XPM, 131
EFS (Encrypting File System), 69–73
  compared to BitLocker Drive Encryption,
      65
  creating certificates, 71
  importing certificates, 73
encryption
  BitLocker Drive Encryption, 64–68
  Encrypting File System, 69–73
Enterprise edition, 2
equations
  Math Input Panel, 103
essential applications (see Windows Live
      Essentials suite)

F

Family Safety, 89
Favorites
  searching in Address bar, 110
features (see new features)
File Sharing, 37–51
  HomeGroup, 37–47
  with Windows XP, 47–49
  with Mac OS X, 50
files, 37
  (see also File Sharing)
  certificates for encrypting, 71
  Encrypting File System, 69–73
filesystems
  BitLocker requirements, 66
filtering
  InPrivate Filtering, 123
  SmartScreen Filter, 128

XXS Filter, 129
filters
    Windows Live Family Safety, 90
find on page feature
    IE8, 113
firewalls
    Windows Firewall, 75
folders
    and libraries, 26–31
    pinning to taskbar, 157
    viewing shared folders, 49

G

gadgets
    about, 15
    displaying on desktop, 31–34
grouping
    IE8, 110

H

hand gestures
    touchscreen support, 150
hibernation
    powercfg tool, 160
    restarting virtual machines, 134
History
    searching in Address bar, 110
Home Basic edition, 2
Home Premium edition, 2
HomeGroup, 37–47
    creating, 39–43
    joining, 43
    sharing files, 43
    sharing printers, 43
    streaming music, 46
Hotmail, naming of, 82
    (see also Windows Live Hotmail; Windows
    Live Mail)

I

icons
    Action Center, 53
    taskbar, 153
IDs
    linking online, 61
IE7 (Internet Explorer 7)
    compatibility with websites and intranet
        pages, 112

IE8 (Internet Explorer 8), 109–130
    accelerators, 120
    Address bar, 110
    Compatibility View, 112
    find on page feature, 113
    grouping, 110
    pinning destinations, 26
    privacy, 121–127
    search, 114
    security, 127–129
    tabbed browsing, 110
    thumbnails, 20
    Web Slices, 116–119
images, burning disk images, 99, 162
    (see also photos)
IMG images
    Windows Disc Image Burner, 99
importing
    certificates, 73
InPrivate Browsing
    IE8, 121
InPrivate Filtering
    IE8, 121, 123
installing
    Linux OS, 138
    printer drivers, 44
    Windows 7, 4–9, 167–175
    XPM, 131–134
Internet Connection Firewall (see Windows
    Firewall)
Internet Explorer (see IE7; IE8)
intranet pages
    compatibility with IE8, 112
ISO images
    burning, 99, 162

J

joining
    HomeGroup, 43
Jump Lists, 22–26

K

keyboard shortcuts
    Areo Snap, 14

L

Libraries
    about, 26–31, 143

sharing, 40, 41, 43
linking
    online IDs, 61
Linux OS
    installing, 138–140
locations
    themes, 148

M

Mac OS X
    Dock feature, 21
    file sharing with, 50
mail
    Windows Live Mail, 81–87
maintenance
    messages about, 53
maps
    searching for, 120
Math Input Panel, 103
Media Center, 101
media players
    Windows Media Player, 107
messages
    maintenance and security, 53
Messenger, 80
Microsoft AntiSpyware (see Windows
        Defender)
Microsoft Surface applications, 11
Microsoft Touch Pack for Windows
    availability, 11
Microsoft Virtual PC 2007, 132
mounting
    ISO images, 101
Movie Maker, 91
multitouch
    support for, 11
music
    streaming, 46

N

netbooks
    installing Windows 7, 167
networks
    wireless, 38
new features, 9–17
    Aero Peek, Aero Shake and Aero Snap, 13
    Calculator, 16
    gadgets, 15, 31–34

Paint and WordPad, 15
Show desktop shortcut, 12
taskbar, 11, 19–26
touchscreen support, 11
Web Slices, 116–119
newsgroups
    subscribing to, 82
notification balloons
    Action Center, 55
NTFS Encryption (see EFS)

O

opening
    command windows, 147
Outlook Express (see Windows Live Mail)

P

Paint, 15, 107
parental control
    Windows Live Family Safety, 89
partitions
    BitLocker operating system encryption, 66
passwords
    HomeGroup, 40
    saving, 60
peeking at the desktop feature, 12
performance
    tests results, 3
Personalize option
    Starter Edition, 2
.pfx certificates
    importing, 73
phishing sites
    SmartScreen Filter, 128
Photo Gallery, 87
Photo Viewer, 97
photos
    Windows Live Photo Gallery, 87
    Windows Photo Viewer, 97
pinning
    applications to the taskbar, 21
    folders to taskbar, 157
Power Policy Configuration tool, 160
powercfg tool
    hibernation, 160
PowerShell, 95–97
printers
    sharing, 37, 43

privacy, 53
   (see also security)
   IE8, 121–127
   Suggested Sites, 127
private folders
   in libraries, 27
Problems Steps Recorder, 158
Professional edition, 2
projector screen selection, 157
public folders
   in libraries, 27

Q

Quick Launch bar, 153

R

RAM requirements, 3
requirements
   drive formatting for BitLocker, 66
   RAM, 3
   system requirements, 3
   video cards for Windows Photo Gallery, 91
restarting virtual machines, 134
restoring Windows Vault, 64
RSS Feeds
   searching in Address bar, 110

S

screen-capture
   Snipping Tool, 92
seamless mode
   Windows XP applications, 136
search
   IE8, 114
security, 53–77
   (see also privacy)
   Action Center, 53–55
   BitLocker Drive Encryption, 64–68
   Credential Manager, 59–64
   Encrypting File System, 69–73
   IE8, 127–129
   shared libraries, 41
   shared printer drivers, 44
   UAC, 57
   Windows Defender, 73
   Windows Firewall, 75
   Windows Live Family Safety, 89
Security Center (see UAC)

shaking active windows, 14
sharing
   calendars, 84
   files, 47–50
   libraries, 41
   printer drivers, 44
shells
   Windows PowerShell, 95–97
short cuts
   Areo Snap keyboard shortcuts, 14
shortcuts
   taskbar shortcuts, 154
   Window key shortcuts, 154
Show desktop shortcut, 12
Sleep Mode
   troubleshooting, 159
SmartScreen Filter
   IE8, 128
Snipping Tool, 92
Sound Recorder, 94
spyware
   Windows Defender, 73
standards-compliance
   IE8, 112
Start menu, 11
   displaying Libraries, 147
   Jump Lists, 23
   legacy applications on Virtual Windows XP, 135
Starter Edition
   HomeGroup, 39
   Windows 7, 2
Sticky Notes, 105
streaming
   music, 46
subscribing
   to calendars, 86
   to newsgroups, 82
Suggested Sites
   IE8, 125
synchronizing
   Calendar and Windows Live Mail, 85
system requirements, 3
system tray
   Action Center, 53

T

tabbed browsing
   IE8, 110

taskbar, 152–157
    about, 11
    Aero Peek, 20
    icons, 153
    Jump Lists, 22–26
    pinning applications to, 21
    pinning folders to, 157
    Quick Launch bar, 153
    shortcuts, 154
tasks
    Jump Lists, 23
themes
    locations, 148
thumb drives
    BitLocker To Go, 67
thumbnails
    of open windows, 20
touchscreen support
    about, 11
    hand gestures, 150
TPM chip
    BitLocker Drive Encryption, 66
troubleshooting
    Sleep Mode, 159
    using Action Center, 54

U

UAC (User Account Control), 57
Ubuntu Linux OS
    installing, 138
UI (User Interface)
    customizing, 143–152
Ultimate edition, 2
upgrading
    from Vista or XP, 4
usability
    IE8, 109–121
USB hard drives
    installing Windows 7, 167–170
USB Mode
    XPM, 137
USB printers
    sharing, 37
USB thumb drives
    installing Windows 7, 170
User Account Control (UAC), 57
User Interface (UI)
    customizing, 143–152

V

vault
    Windows Vault, 59
versions (see editions of Windows 7)
VHD files
    installing Windows 7 on, 172–175
video cards
    Windows Photo Gallery requirements, 91
videos
    Windows Live Movie Maker, 91
Virtual Windows XP, 132
Vista (see Windows Vista)
visual search
    IE8, 114

W

Web Slices
    IE8, 116–119
Window key shortcuts, 154
Windows 7 Compatibility Mode, 164
Windows Defender, 73
Windows Disc Image Burner, 99
Windows Easy Transfer, 4
Windows Explorer
    default view, 143
Windows Firewall, 75
Windows Live Essentials suite, 79–92
    Windows Live Family Safety, 89
    Windows Live Mail, 81–87
    Windows Live Messenger, 80
    Windows Live Movie Maker, 91
    Windows Live Photo Gallery, 87
    Windows Live Writer, 88
Windows Live Family Safety, 89
Windows Live Hotmail
    Credential Manager, 60
    naming of, 82
Windows Live Mail
    about, 81–87
    Calendar, 84–87
    naming of, 82
    newsgroups, 82
    synchronizing with Calendar, 85
Windows Live Messenger, 80
Windows Live Movie Maker, 91
Windows Live Photo Gallery, 87
Windows Live Writer, 88
Windows Media Center, 101

Windows Media Player, 107
Windows Movie Maker, 91
Windows Photo Gallery, 87
Windows Photo Viewer, 97
Windows PowerShell, 95–97
Windows Sidebar, 31
Windows Vault
    credentials, 59
Windows Virtual PC
    installing other operating systems, 138
Windows Vista
    dual booting, 171–172
    upgrading from, 4
Windows XP
    dual booting, 171–172
    sharing files with, 47–49
    upgrading from, 4
Windows XP Mode (see XPM)
wireless networks
    connecting to, 38
WordPad, 15, 107
worksheets
    Calculator, 106
Writer, 88

X

XP (see Windows XP)
XPM (Windows XP Mode), 131–142
    installing, 131–134
    installing other operating systems, 138–
        140
    running in Windows 7, 135–137
XPS (XML Paper Specification)
    defined, 104
XPS Document Writer, 105
XPS Viewer, 104
XSS filter, 129

About the Author

Wei-Meng Lee (Microsoft MVP) is a technologist and founder of Developer Learning Solutions (*http://www.learn2develop.net*), a technology company specializing in hands-on training for the latest Microsoft and Apple technologies.

Wei-Meng speaks regularly at international conferences and has authored and coauthored many books on .NET, XML, and wireless technologies. He writes extensively on topics ranging from .NET to Mac OS X. He is also the author of *Windows XP Unwired* and *.NET Compact Framework Pocket Guide*, both from O'Reilly.

Colophon

The animal on the cover of *Windows 7: Up and Running* is a Persian greyhound (*Canis familiaris*), known more commonly today as a saluki. Scientists believe the Persian greyhound is the earliest known breed of domesticated dog; DNA analysis identifies this dog as one of the first to have diverged from wolves.

Persian greyhound–like animals decorate Iranian ceramics from 3500 BC and Egyptian tombs from 2100 BC; the Persian greyhound also inspired Alberto Giacometti's 1951 surrealist sculpture titled "Dog". The breed gained an enormous following in England in the late 1800s when the Honorable Florence Amherst imported a pair of Persian greyhounds from Egypt and bred them. The Persian greyhound became popular in the United States soon after.

While some are turned off by the breed's aloofness and tendency toward boredom when given repetitive tasks, many children love the Persian greyhound because it is gentle with them. The dog's gentle nature can disappear quickly, however, when it ventures outside and spots an animal it believes is prey. Veterinarians recommend that the dog never go off-leash outdoors, as it is nearly impossible to train the the Persian greyhound to suppress its hunting instinct.

The cover image is from Lydekker's *Royal Natural History*. The cover font is Adobe ITC Garamond. The text font is Linotype Birka; the heading font is Adobe Myriad Condensed; and the code font is LucasFont's TheSansMonoCondensed.

Get even more
for your money.

Join the O'Reilly Community, and register the O'Reilly books you own.It's free, and you'll get:

- 40% upgrade offer on O'Reilly books
- Membership discounts on books and events
- Free lifetime updates to electronic formats of books
- Multiple ebook formats, DRM FREE
- Participation in the O'Reilly community
- Newsletters
- Account management
- 100% Satisfaction Guarantee

Signing up is easy:

1. **Go to: oreilly.com/go/register**
2. **Create an O'Reilly login.**
3. **Provide your address.**
4. **Register your books.**

Note: English-language books only

To order books online:

oreilly.com/order_new

For questions about products or an order:

orders@oreilly.com

To sign up to get topic-specific email announcements and/or news about upcoming books, conferences, special offers, and new technologies:

elists@oreilly.com

For technical questions about book content:

booktech@oreilly.com

To submit new book proposals to our editors:

proposals@oreilly.com

Many O'Reilly books are available in PDF and several ebook formats. For more information:

oreilly.com/ebooks

O'REILLY®

Spreading the knowledge of innovators

www.oreilly.com

Buy this book and get access to the online edition for 45 days—for free!

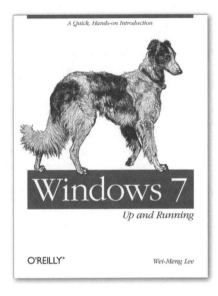

Windows 7: Up and Running
By Wei-Meng Lee
September 2009, $24.99
ISBN 9780596804046

With Safari Books Online, you can:

Access the contents of thousands of technology and business books

- Quickly search over 7000 books and certification guides
- Download whole books or chapters in PDF format, at no extra cost, to print or read on the go
- Copy and paste code
- Save up to 35% on O'Reilly print books
- **New!** Access mobile-friendly books directly from cell phones and mobile devices

Stay up-to-date on emerging topics before the books are published

- Get on-demand access to evolving manuscripts.
- Interact directly with authors of upcoming books

Explore thousands of hours of video on technology and design topics

- Learn from expert video tutorials
- Watch and replay recorded conference sessions

To try out Safari and the online edition of this book FREE for 45 days, go to *www.oreilly.com/go/safarienabled* and enter the coupon code VVBRIWH. To see the complete Safari Library, visit safari.oreilly.com.